Disadvantage

KEYWORDS IN TEACHER EDUCATION

Series Editor: Viv Ellis

Taking cultural theorist Raymond Williams's concept as an organizing device, the **Keywords in Teacher Education** series offers short, accessibly written books on the most pressing and challenging ideas in the field.

Teacher education has a high profile in public policy and professional debates given the enduring associations between how teachers are prepared and how well their students do in school. At the same time, research perspectives on the important topics in the field are increasingly polarized with important consequences for the kind of teacher and the qualities of teaching that are most valued. Written by internationally recognized experts, these titles offer analyses both of the historical emergence and the consequences of the different positions in these debates.

Also available in the Series:

Expertise, Jessica Gerrard and Jessica Holloway
Identity, Sarah Steadman
Quality, Clare Brooks
Communities, Kenneth M. Zeichner

Forthcoming in the Series:

Knowledge, Steven Puttick, Victoria Elliott and Jenni Ingram

Disadvantage

**JO LAMPERT
MERVI KAUKKO
JANE WILKINSON
ROCÍO GARCÍA-CARRIÓN**

BLOOMSBURY ACADEMIC
LONDON • NEW YORK • OXFORD • NEW DELHI • SYDNEY

BLOOMSBURY ACADEMIC
Bloomsbury Publishing Plc
50 Bedford Square, London, WC1B 3DP, UK
1385 Broadway, New York, NY 10018, USA
29 Earlsfort Terrace, Dublin 2, Ireland

BLOOMSBURY, BLOOMSBURY ACADEMIC and the
Diana logo are trademarks of Bloomsbury Publishing Plc

First published in Great Britain 2024

Cover design: Charlotte James
Cover image © Zoonar GmbH / Alamy Stock Photo

A catalogue record for this book is available from the British Library.

A catalog record for this book is available from the Library of Congress.

ISBN: HB: 978-1-3502-5910-2
        PB: 978-1-3502-5909-6
        ePDF: 978-1-3502-5911-9
        eBook: 978-1-3502-5912-6

Series: Keywords in Teacher Education

Typeset by Integra Software Services Pvt. Ltd.
Printed and bound in Great Britain

To find out more about our authors and books visit www.bloomsbury.com
and sign up for our newsletters.

CONTENTS

TABLES

SERIES EDITOR'S FOREWORD

This series is organized by the concept of "keywords," first elaborated by Welsh cultural theorist Raymond Williams (1976), and books in the series will seek to problematize and unsettle the ostensibly unproblematic and settled vocabulary of teacher education. From Williams's perspective, keywords are words and phrases that occur frequently in speech and writing, allowing conversation to ensue, but that nonetheless reveal profound differences in meaning within and across cultures, politics, and histories. In teacher education, such keywords include practice, knowledge, quality, and expertise. The analysis of such keywords allows us to trace the evolution of the emergent—and the maintenance of residual—meanings in teacher education discourses and practices. By analyzing keywords, therefore, it is possible to elucidate the range of meanings of what Gallie (1955) referred to as "essentially contested concepts" but in ways that promote a critical, historical understanding of changes in the fields in which they occur.

In the first edition of *Keywords*, Williams included entries on 108 units, ranging from "Aesthetic" to "Work." A second edition followed in 1983 and other writers have subsequently used the concept to expand on Williams's original collection (e.g., Bennett et al., 2005; MacCabe & Yanacek, 2018) or to apply the concept to specific domains (e.g., A Community of Inquiry, 2018). This series applies it to teacher education. The purpose of the series mirrors that of Williams's original project: to trace ideological differences and social conflicts over time as they relate to the discourses and practices of a field (here, teacher education) by focusing on a selection of the field's high-frequency words. So *Keywords in Teacher Education* is not a multi-volume dictionary.

The kind of analysis required by a focus on keywords goes beyond etymology or historical semantics. By selecting and analyzing keywords, Williams argued:

> we find a history and complexity of meanings; conscious changes, or consciously different uses; innovation, obsolescence, specialization, extension, overlap, transfer; or changes which are masked by a nominal continuity so that words which seem to have been there for centuries, with continuous general meanings, have come in fact to express radically different or radically variable, yet sometimes hardly noticed, meanings and implications of meaning.
>
> (Williams, 1976, p. 17)

Given the increasingly strong attention paid to teacher education in education policy and in public debates about education more generally, focusing on keywords in this field is both timely and necessary. Uncovering and unsettling differences and conflicts in the vocabulary of preparing teachers renders the political and social bases underlying policy formation and public discourse more visible and therefore more capable of being acted upon.

Through this organizing device, the *Keywords in Teacher Education* series addresses the most important topics and questions in teacher education currently. It is a series of short books written in a direct and accessible style, each book taking one keyword as its point of departure and closely examining its cultural meanings historically whilst, crucially, identifying the social forces and material consequences of the differences and conflicts in meaning. Written by internationally recognized researchers, each peer-reviewed book offers cutting-edge analysis of the keyword underpinned by a deep knowledge of the available research within the field—and beyond it. One of the aims of the series is to broaden the gaze of teacher education research by engaging more systematically with the relevant humanities and social science literature—to acknowledge, as Williams did, that our understanding is deepened and potential for action strengthened by seeking to understand the social relations between words, texts, and the multiple contexts in which their meanings are produced.

In this brilliant contribution to the series, Lampert, Wilkinson, and Kaukko explore the keyword *disadvantage*, one which, as the authors put it, "seems self-explanatory on the surface, is itself troublesome." The authors show how, since the 1960s, the idea of education as "compensation" for disadvantage has become commonplace, with specific forms of education tailored to the needs of the category "the disadvantaged." As Ellis, Gatti, and Mansell (2023) show, since the Global Financial Crisis of 2008, the importance attached to how teachers are prepared for public (i.e., state-funded) schools has accelerated, with the notion of "teaching quality" becoming a key policy tool for governments to tackle structural, economic disadvantage and to promote "social mobility," despite simultaneously imposing austerity measures and cutting public service budgets. Consequently, disadvantage has become even more important as a keyword in teacher education as universities and other providers are now expected to prepare teachers who can address structural economic and social problems—and are responsibilized for doing so—as well as teaching children and young people well. In policy discourses from multiple political perspectives, teacher education has come to be seen as a primary means of tackling disadvantage just as much as it is a means of developing good teachers.

A great strength of this book is how the authors navigate the complexities of meanings for disadvantage and the effects of these meanings. Inequality and inequities are real; societies are riven by injustices, historical, and contemporary. Education—and teacher education especially, with its powerful reproductive intent—has a part to play in addressing these injustices by interrupting those reproductions. But how can we avoid falling into the trap of deficit thinking? What does it mean to understand disadvantage as plural, relative, and intersectional? What can we learn from past and present examples of forms of teacher education motivated by the ideals of social justice? Lampert and her colleagues address these questions and many others that invite us to think—as Williams would have appreciated—what other words we would use in its place. They conclude with considerations of the Marxist and Freirean concepts of praxis and hope and, through accounts of the innovative work of teachers and teacher educators, show what new forms of transformative teacher education may look like.

Viv Ellis
Melbourne, 2023

References

A Community of Inquiry (2018). *Keywords; for further consideration and particularly relevant to academic life, especially as it concerns disciplines, inter-disciplinary endeavor and modes of resistance to the same*. Princeton, NJ: Princeton University Press.

Bennett, T., Grossberg, L., & Morris, M. (2005). *New keywords. A revised vocabulary of culture and society*. Oxford: Blackwell Publishing.

Ellis, V., Gatti, L., & Mansell, W. (2023). *The new political economy of teacher education: The enterprise narrative and the shadow state*. Bristol: Policy Press.

Ericsson, K.A., Krampe, R.T., & Tesch-Romer, C. (1993). The role of deliberate practice in the acquisition of expert performance. *Psychological Review*, 100(3): 363–406.

Gallie, W. B. (1955). Essentially contested concepts. *Proceedings of the Aristotelian Society*, 56: 167–98.

McCabe, C., Yanacek, H., & the Keywords Project (2018). *Keywords for today. A 21st century vocabulary*. Oxford: Oxford University Press.

Williams, R. (1976). *Keywords: A vocabulary of culture and society*. London, UK: Fontana.

CHAPTER ONE

Introducing *Disadvantage*

Introduction

Most teacher education programs across the globe include at least some curriculum to prepare teachers to understand the educational effects of disadvantage. Social and economic disadvantage is globally recognized by significant international groups such as UNESCO, Amnesty International, and the Organisation for Economic Co-operation and Development (OECD) as having significant impact on students' educational outcomes. However, the word *disadvantage*, which seems self-explanatory on the surface, is itself troublesome. While some educational theory and many educational policies often refer to the effects of educational disadvantage, many school leaders, teachers, students, and historically marginalized communities dislike the word disadvantage, sometimes intensely. This book is unique in its examination of the discursive uses of the term disadvantage in teacher education. This is very different from books that explain disadvantage or offer strategies to address it. Instead, we interrogate the keyword itself, with two aims: to examine how teacher educators could use the term more reflexively in their own teaching and to encourage preservice teachers to do the same.

Though it is contested, the word disadvantage is commonly used in teacher education across many nations and in social policy. Examining disadvantage is recognized as important critical work that teachers must undertake to become democratic teachers who are agents of social change (Nuttall & Beckett, 2020). Recognizing disadvantage is seen as crucial in preparing socially just teachers who can identify and address inequities. Coupled with its discursive partners, inclusion, and diversity, preservice teachers in the Global North are generally asked to engage with theories of disadvantage and advised to recognize, support, and lead change for students who historically experience high levels of exclusion and marginalization.

At face value, naming disadvantage is crucial in making inequities visible. For instance, preservice teachers need to understand how the unequal distribution of resources results in students from middle-class or wealthier backgrounds having substantially more opportunities. However, preservice teachers also need the critical tools to deconstruct or unpack how students from some backgrounds are represented and misrepresented. Informed by Nancy Fraser (1997), these two issues of distribution and representation are—or should be—central concepts in initial teacher education.

So how could we possibly overcome (or even overthrow) injustice without naming disadvantage? Surely, even if we dislike the word itself, we will not want to obscure the fact that injustice in education exists, especially for young people from historically marginalized communities. Let us not pretend that everyone receives an equal or equitable education. On the other hand, the risk is that we construct, possibly unwittingly, one imaginary category we call "the disadvantaged."

Calling disadvantage out is crucial in highlighting the need to redistribute resources and to prepare just and democratic teachers who can recognize and address these inequities (Heimans et al., 2021). However, without historical or critical context, the use of the word disadvantage becomes a kind of truth claim, despite its complexity. Sensoy and DiAngelo (2017) refer to words such as disadvantage as "Trojan Horse terms": They might seem helpful at first glance, but rather than promoting equity, they may end up causing more harm than good. Discourses of disadvantage may indeed reproduce disadvantage (Hayes et al., 2008), by promoting stereotypes and alienating the very people they purport to help. Discourses can also portray schools in disadvantaged areas in a homogenizing manner and assume that all such schools share similar challenges related to socioeconomic disadvantage and ethnic diversity (Peltola et al., 2023, p. 212). The vocabulary of disadvantage is, as Williams suggests, one of those words whose meaning is inextricably bound up with the problems it is used to discuss (Williams, 1985, p. 14). Nevertheless, rendering disadvantage invisible cannot be the answer.

In this introductory chapter and in the subsequent chapters in this book we present an overview of the word disadvantage to untangle how its meaning is variously constructed in context-based, politically constituted, and sometimes contradictory ways. We take the position that the word disadvantage can *both* help or hinder, empower or disempower, liberate or oppress, promote democracy or reproduce inequities.

What Do We Mean by Disadvantage?

As Kellaghan (2001) notes, the use of the word disadvantage is often broad and inadequate, something that Gazeley (2019, p. 685) suggests makes it a difficult construct to work with. Smit (2012) argues that "Disadvantage has become an umbrella term to cover a wide array of perceived shortcomings and has not been clearly conceptualised" (p. 370). Functionally, words such as disadvantage aim to identify those worst off and take appropriate steps so that their position can be improved. However, some critical questions remain: "What do we mean by disadvantage? And how can that ever be measured?" (Bibby et al., 2017, p. 108). How can it be addressed, as it functions on so many levels (Bernelius & Kosunen, 2023, 187) and "Is this meaning shared?" (Spring, 2007, p. 3).

Indeed, many educators, including teachers and principals, are uncomfortable with the word disadvantage, finding it stigmatizing and unproductive because of its focus on deficits. For instance, school leaders know that working in a school known as disadvantaged affects the morale of students and teachers; furthermore, such a reputation also affects school enrolments because middle-class parents choose to send their children to schools without this stigma. Students labeled as disadvantaged find the stereotype a significant barrier to their achievement (Fuligni, 2007). Young people in so-called disadvantaged schools know that is their label, as do their families, and both often experience stigma and shame associated with being called disadvantaged (Thompson & Mentor, 2017, p. 33), something we discuss in subsequent chapters. However, discourses of disadvantage are still regularly used, sometimes ubiquitously, both in educational policy and by educators. Though school leaders often see it as derogatory, the word disadvantage continues to come through in policy, even when other words or terminology are claimed as preferred. Clearly, disadvantage is a hard word to replace without resorting to euphemism and generic word substitutes. Calling a school "diverse," "challenging," or even "high poverty" or "hard to staff" can obscure the historical disadvantage that more aptly sums up the experiences of vulnerable young people and their families.

When Did Disadvantage Emerge in Educational Policy?

The word disadvantage did not come "out of nowhere" (Gorur, 2011, p. 613): It has pervaded educational policy since the 1960s. During the long period of time during which the vocabulary of disadvantage has become taken-for-granted,

> We find a history and complexity of meanings, conscious changes, or consciously different uses; innovation,

obsolescence, specialization, extension, overlap, transfer; or changes which are masked by a nominal continuity so that words that seem to have been there for centuries, with continuous general meanings, have come in fact to express radically different, or radically variable yet sometimes hardly noticed, meanings and implications of meaning.

(Williams, 1985, p. 16)

Associated with social reform, the term "educational disadvantage" began to appear in policy in the United States in the 1960s to propose "compensatory" school policy and strategies (Smith & Smith, 2014). Over time, compensatory educational policies and interventions have become known in the UK as area-based initiatives (ABIs) (Raffo, 2011). In Australia, sociologist Raewyn Connell and colleagues' significant and influential Disadvantaged Schools Program (DSP) ran from 1974 to 1990 (Connell et al., 1992). We use these few examples to illustrate how the word disadvantage has served a particular aim and has often been a productive lens through which to understand and address inequities. Addressing educational disadvantage has been an important measure in supporting young people to "climb the ladder of opportunity" that has been withheld from them (Power et al., 2010, p. 23).

Many educational policies have been, and are still, formulated on theories of disadvantage. These policies emphasize the roles schools play in addressing the impact of disadvantage on students and families and are also generally careful to note the multidimensional nature of disadvantage, striving, with varying degrees of success, not to equate disadvantage with poverty. For instance, while poverty is a large measure of disadvantage, it would be reasonably rare now to read policy that suggests poverty can be untangled from other dimensions of disadvantage. In Australia, McLachlan et al.'s (2013) report for Australia's Productivity Commission takes good care to explain the multidimensional nature of disadvantage, as do the regular reports produced by Australia's Brotherhood of St. Laurence (Phillips & Narayanan, 2020). These reports are careful in explaining that

> Disadvantage has its roots in a complex interplay of factors. Many of these factors, when combined, can have a compounding effect. The probability that any one person will experience disadvantage is influenced by: their personal capabilities and family circumstances; the support they receive; the community where they live (and the opportunities it offers); life events; and the broader economic and social environment.
>
> (McLachlan et al., 2013, p. 12)

The report from the Committee for Economic Development of Australia (2015) emphasizes the complexities of historic and relative poverty, pointing to specific concerns about how disadvantage is historically entrenched for groups of people such as those with disabilities, people from non-English-speaking backgrounds, elderly Australians and, most significantly, Indigenous Australians. The language of disadvantage is used in both the report for the Australian Council of Social Service (Davidson et al., 2020) and the *Closing the Gap* report (Australian Government, 2020), which has been published annually since 2009 and details progress on closing the health and life expectancy gap between Indigenous and non-Indigenous Australians.

Discourses of disadvantage are present in educational policy throughout the Global North. For instance, in the UK, the pupil premium, which started in 2011, identified criteria to target young people deemed to be disadvantaged (Bibby et al., 2017). In the United States, the National School Lunch Program provides money for schools serving disadvantaged communities (Cheng & Peterson, 2021), and in Australia, the Gonski Review (Gonski et al., 2018) drove policy to provide specific additional funding to disadvantaged schools. Hiding disadvantage behind less explicit language could disrupt much-needed initiatives intended to even out the playing field. As Becky Francis (cited in Bibby et al., 2017) states, "It [meaning calling out disadvantage where it is present] forces schools to attend to materially benefiting those pupils from low SES [socioeconomic status] backgrounds, and cannot be monopolised by, or redirected to, their more affluent peers" (p. 100). Despite debates about whether disadvantage is the best word to use, it is generally used to advocate for social change (for example, when used by charities such as The Smith Family in Australia) and can be useful in leveraging funding for important social justice work.

However, disadvantage is a very broad catchphrase, and its use risks reductionism or simplification. Most contemporary theories and policy recognize that disadvantage is plural rather than relative or absolute, or simply monetary. Attempts to provide more nuanced definitions of disadvantage include explanations of compound or multiple disadvantages (for instance, the cumulative effects of poverty + poor health + underemployment + low educational attainment), relative disadvantage (disadvantage in relation to others in one's own geographical or community context), community disadvantage (for instance, being new to, or ostracized within, a community, having few or weak social networks or opportunities), and social disadvantage (such as being alienated or isolated—for instance, because of one's gender or sexuality).

Disadvantage is still the most used catch-all descriptor to describe inequity in education. This is despite education policy writers generally being careful to acknowledge that disadvantage is not merely economic. It is more common now to use terms such as *social inclusion* or *social exclusion* than to find discourses strictly related to social class. Disadvantage-related inequities have been exacerbated by the COVID-19 pandemic, increasing attention to the word disadvantage as school leaders, teachers, teacher educators, and policymakers note the widening chasms between communities and how they have been impacted by the pandemic. Communities already experiencing complex and historical disadvantage have been drastically affected by everything from a lack of digital access for online learning, crisis-level teacher shortages in certain schools, and health and mortality within low socioeconomic and culturally diverse communities. One can anticipate an increased and increasingly complex discourse related to the concept of disadvantage.

Why Are Some People Bothered by the Word Disadvantage?

Disadvantage has become an everyday or "familiar term," but it still has effects—intended and otherwise—on the people it describes (McLeod & Wright, 2016, p. 777). Indeed, it is a "significant, binding word" (Williams, 1985, p. 15) in the field of education. And because disadvantage itself is a construct, the word disadvantage can syntactically be used in various ways. Spring (2007) suggests that any word beginning with the prefix *dis* (such as disadvantage, disempowered, dismissed) negates or reverses a positive activity (p. 4). Definitions of poverty and disadvantage change over time as geo-political boundaries shift, populations relocate and the ways in census data is collected are revised. In the UK, Smith & Smith (2014) have traced how definitions of both poverty and disadvantage have shifted since the 1960s when policies directed toward educational disadvantage were first put in place. In Australia, the United States and Canada there is a current policy shift away from referring to groups of people as "the disadvantaged" to writing about "historical disadvantage" or people who "experience disadvantage." In general, we no longer refer to anyone as "the disadvantaged" as though this is an attribute or a trait. It is best to understand disadvantage as a condition that is historically imposed rather than an identity, a character flaw, or a situation of one's own making. The linguistic shift is sometimes fuzzy and inconsistent.

Tension is often present in policy that confuses what is the fault of the individual and what is historical. For example, this tension can be seen in a recent issues paper entitled "What is Community Disadvantage" (Price-Robertson, 2021), which explains that

> Community disadvantage emerges out of the interplay between the characteristics of the residents in a community (e.g., employment, education levels, drug and alcohol use) and, over and above this, the effects of the social and environmental context in which they exist (i.e., "place effects" or "neighbourhood effects", such as weak social networks, poor role models and a relative lack of opportunity).
>
> (p. 2)

In this statement, we still see a tangible trace of negative discourses, a palimpsest that still supposes disadvantage is the result of personal flaws or character deficits.

Unpacking teachers' beliefs about the causes and subsequent strategies to address disadvantage has been the focus of much research. Many teachers, and indeed, teacher educators, hold on to deficit beliefs that directly or indirectly imply that individuals cause their own disadvantage. The deficit "character flaw" construct is alive and present. For example, Ruby Payne's poverty framework, which gained enormous traction in the Global North, is a popular professional development program for teachers that is often criticized for outlining for teachers the personal characteristics of poor people, confusing historical disadvantage with personal attributes. Payne's explanations for poverty or disadvantage, offered to teachers in a series of workshops, are an example of how disadvantage is still problematically defined through

> perceived behavioural shortcomings—things like [people's] lack of commitment to improving their situation, indifferent motivation generally, unlawful conduct, and parents'

inadequate attention to child rearing. Indeed, surface appearances of the kinds mentioned are used to justify a view that the dominant cause of residents' plight resides in their moral slackness and own defective personal choices.

(Vinson, 2009, p. 4)

Indeed, the term "disadvantage" itself is seen by some as contributing to a politics of blame. And yet, as Smyth (2012) explains, "The more we refuse to understand the history of how people come to experience disadvantage and what keeps them that way, then the more we are susceptible to the snake oil put around by people like Ruby Payne" (p. 11). There is a long history of intentionally or unintentionally demonizing the very people we claim to serve. This includes missionary perspectives and the subjectification of certain groups as worthy of pity, which some refer to as "poverty porn" (Wrigley, 2019, p. 154).

As UK scholars Bibby, Lupton, and Raffo (2017) write, educational policies tend to write out the realities of the lives of disadvantaged children and families both in the sense of the ways they manifest in the classroom and in the sense of their impact on educational outcomes. While the reality that some students are disadvantaged by school systems is undeniable, there are serious concerns about the deficit understandings produced or constructed by disadvantage discourses. Nobody wants to obscure discussions of inequity, but there are two main and serious concerns about the use of the word. One is the deeply engrained assumptions that may be held about why people are disadvantaged. The other related concern is that deficit beliefs (such as that some parents disadvantage their own children by not caring about education) lead to solutions based on deficit or lack (for example, that teachers need to counteract or compensate for the harm done by these parents). As an example, there has been regular criticism of the Australian Government's *Closing the Gap* report. While no one would dispute that inequities still exist and that Indigenous and non-Indigenous students must have equal education, the *Closing the Gap* report is often criticized for focusing just on despair, obscuring healthy, strong, and proud Indigenous people.

Australian Aboriginal scholar Kerry Arabena (2017) explains her dislike of the word disadvantage from an Indigenous perspective, pointing out how language affects our thinking. Arabena argues that there is an important difference between defining disadvantage as an identity (the disadvantaged) versus an experience (of having been disadvantaged). Arabena writes, "I long for the day when I don't have to sell a deficit story to get $$$" (final para). And yet racism, poverty, and inequality remain as strong as ever, despite all that funding. Arabena's point is that "disadvantage" becomes a defining, even a "market-driven," identity. She explains why there is resistance from Indigenous communities to a word that has led to such little change.

In fact, the term "educational disadvantage" is so heavily coded, tentative, and controversial that it is often used with scare marks around it to indicate that it is being used nervously and even, sometimes, ironically. This is the case for Australian Indigenous scholar Melitta Hogarth (2017) who cannot avoid the use of the word disadvantage but makes her opinion of it known through her ironic quotation marks. Aboriginal academic Marnee Shay and colleagues (Shay et al., 2019) recorded the voices of Aboriginal youth to write the *Imagination Declaration*, and those young people explicitly state in writing that they do not want to be defined through the lens of disadvantage. In the Global South, we also find indigenous students in Mexico who have reacted against the stigma of disadvantage calling for an identity that does not exclude them (Flores-Crespo, 2007). Indigenous mixed methods defined by the indigenous scholar Bagele Chilisa from Botswana provide us with a framework that problematizes, critiques, and challenges what have historically excluded people named as "disadvantaged" (Chilisa & Tsheko, 2014).

Personal Experiences of Being Called Disadvantaged

Obviously, disadvantage is a discursive construction that carries judgmental overtones exacerbated by media that continuously represents "the poor" and "the disadvantaged" as morally suspect and the cause of their own problems (Fincher & Saunders, 2020, p. 5). Those who have the lived experience of disadvantage report that being labeled as such positions them as victims and can be degrading and stigmatizing. Implementing policies about disadvantage can "increase people's feelings of oppressive treatment, powerlessness, and stigmatization, social isolation and at its worst, oppression, exploitation, domination, servility, snobbery and other hierarchical evils" (Wolff & de-Shalit, 2007, p. 5). Even when the act of identifying groups of people as disadvantaged appears to lead to steps that are "taken for their own good and on their own behalf" (Wolff & de-Shalit, 2007, p. 13), there are perils: Well-meaning terms such as disadvantage can backfire. As Williams points out (1985), the complexity of the meaning of words like disadvantage is that they may contribute very little to the resolution of actual class disputes and class struggles (p. 21).

Most concerns about the use of the word disadvantage center on stigma, shame, and especially stereotype. There is plenty of evidence that negative stereotypes held by some new and established teachers about impoverished children can perpetuate inequality. As examples, teachers who have little personal understanding of poverty are often misinformed, have low aspirations for their students, may make unfounded assumptions, and hold deficit views of poverty. There is extensive literature outlining how young people from low socioeconomic backgrounds are detained, expelled, and punished more often. Since disadvantage is intersectional, punitive behavior management has impact on Black students and students from vilified minority groups (Milner, 2013), and there is significant scholarship on how young people from historically vulnerable or marginalized backgrounds are overrepresented in "special education" classes (Zhang et al., 2014).

Disadvantage is most often a term coined not by those who experience it, but by policymakers and well-meaning support people. As such, the word itself mediates how already marginalized people can view themselves. As Spring (2007) writes, "This is a telling example of how language can be used to distance those in powerful positions from those on the margins" (p. 7)—an unintended consequence.

Whether the word disadvantage is favored or not, it is highly unlikely that we would argue that schooling has equal outcomes for everyone. Masking disadvantage—or calling it something else—does not change the poor health, social, and educational outcomes of those who experience it.

Disadvantage: Pros and Cons

The word disadvantage is problematic, often contested, and coded with meaning and thus poses a dilemma to social justice educators who care deeply about inequities in education. Taken-for-granted misconceptions and stereotypes can have profound impacts on students and their families, yet "hiding" disadvantage is not the answer. Instead, educators need better preparation and more opportunities to develop a critical perspective on the contexts of poverty and social disadvantage. Therefore, we suggest that the word disadvantage not be obscured but used more critically.

Like Bibby et al. (2017), we believe that

> poverty and socio-economic disadvantage must continue to be named and spelled out, perhaps for a generation of teachers who … may simply not have been exposed to a more economic, historical, spatialised or sociological account of the individual circumstances that present in their classrooms.
>
> (p. 198)

Not "outing" disadvantage can become a "pedagogy of indifference" (Lingard & Keddie, 2013), so any term we substitute for disadvantage "would have to be more than a 'facile makeover'" (Smyth, 2012, p. 11).

We conclude this chapter with some remaining questions:

1 What is the aim of using the word disadvantage, and who defines it?

2 Would changing the language of disadvantage be transformative or regressive? Would it lead to better practice?

3 Whose purpose does it serve, when, and why?

4 If the word is replaced with something more transformative, what would that be? What would be lost and what would be gained?

CHAPTER TWO

Disadvantage and Intersectionalities

Introduction

*They are damaged, lacking in trust and discipline, and
highly self-interested. But the poor are still a force
that Australia needs to properly harness.*

(Goward, 2021)

The above quotation comes from Pru Goward, a former
minister for family and community services in New South
Wales, the largest state government of Australia. Her
opinion piece entitled "Why You Shouldn't Underestimate
the Underclass" was published in *The Financial Review*, an
Australian newspaper with a national circulation that is read
by senior business and opinion leaders. It came after her
appointment in 2019 as a professor of social interventions and
policy at Western Sydney University (WSU) to lead, among
other projects, the "development of an evidence bank" that
would "provide ground breaking and reliable advice on the
effectiveness of programs designed for the early intervention
and prevention of complex social problems in Australia" (WSU
News Centre, 2021). Condemnation of Goward's opinion

piece was swift. Current and former students at the university, as well as academics, called for her removal. One student summed up the prevailing sentiment of dismay, arguing, "I and many of the students I know started at Western Sydney University to bring ourselves OUT of the cycle of poverty that we were BORN into. We are far from being damaged, lacking in discipline, and self-interested as her article infers" (change. org, n.d., emphasis in original).

That the former minister was appointed to WSU was a particularly bitter pill to swallow for its ethnically diverse student populace. WSU's campuses are in some of the poorest regions of Sydney, areas that service "a large multicultural population of more than two million people" (WSU, n.d.-a). It has one of the largest teacher education faculties in Australia, with many of its teaching graduates being from low socioeconomic and/or highly diverse ethnic backgrounds, who are often the first in family to attend university. Over 90 percent of WSU's undergraduate students are admitted based on alternative criteria to the traditional university admissions ranking, the Australian Tertiary Admission Rank (ATAR; WSU, n.d.-c). WSU's website lists its values as "boldness, fairness, integrity and excellence" (WSU, n.d.-b), an institution where students "from vulnerable groups … can find a sense of belonging" (change.org., n.d.).

Unfortunately, despite being stereotypical and prejudiced, Goward's comments about poverty are neither unsurprising nor original. They sit within a long tradition of stigmatizing policy discourses about poverty in Anglophone nations. These discourses originate, at least in part, from nineteenth-century Victorian England's division of the poor into those who were seen as "deserving" of Christian charity and those who were "undeserving." The latter group was often labeled as undeserving, as noted in Chapter 1, due to a perceived character flaw or a situation of ones' own making such as excessive drug or alcohol consumption. The sense of shame felt by those who are stereotyped through these stigmatizing poverty discourses is suggested in the student's comments quoted above. Additionally, Goward's description of the poor as an "underclass" echoes earlier policy descriptors, by which the poor were lumped together into a collective noun, as if being poor was an "attribute or trait" that one had been born with rather than a condition that is historically imposed.

This chapter examines taken-for-granted assumptions about disadvantage such as those foregrounded by Goward's stereotyping of the poor as a homogenized underclass. It seeks to understand differences in the ways the word is used by local and historically marginalized communities to analyze how these communities define, contest, or engage in debates about disadvantage. It examines these assumptions and differences through the lens of students from diverse African nations who have sought refuge in host nations in the Global North. They are a group who have experienced high levels of stigma, marginalization, and discrimination in these nations due to the intersectionality of their "race," ethnicity, and poverty. Before doing so, however, the chapter begins with a personal reflection on the lived experiences of disadvantage and what this personal history reveals about disadvantage's multidimensional nature. It then examines the origins of intersectionality as a theory to suggest its usefulness when it comes to problematizing previously taken-for-granted assumptions that underlie how disadvantage has been used or misused in teacher education theory and practice.

Personal Reflections on Being "Disadvantaged"

The incoming Labor Prime Minister of Australia declared the following in his party's victory speech:

> It says a lot about our great country that a son of a single mum who was a disability pensioner, who grew up in public housing … can stand before you as Australia's prime minister

... I've been underestimated my whole life [but] I have also
been lifted up by others who saw something in me.

(Albanese, 2022)

Although disadvantaged is not a term that Jane, one of the
coauthors of this book, recalls hearing as a child, the negative
implications of the term were part of her upbringing. These
negative experiences were clearly that of Australia's incoming
Prime Minister Anthony Albanese, whose quotation opens
this section. Like the prime minister, Jane grew up in a poor
family headed by a sole parent who was raising three children
and doing "unskilled" work to support them. Unlike the
prime minister's mother, Jane's mother was a migrant with a
heavy accent from a non-English-speaking background. She
was Jewish in a Christian location where there were very few
others like them. Like many of Australia's postwar migrant
generation, Jane's mum learned English on the factory floor.
She had little formal education. Divorce was highly unusual in
those days. So, there was an added stigma in being a "deserted
wife" without a husband as the main breadwinner. As children
of such parents Jane and her sisters unconsciously absorbed
that stigma and sense of shame.

Jane completed her education at the Australian equivalent
of a comprehensive government high school. It was poorly
funded, had large class sizes, and was full of first-year
teachers, some of whom were trained in the progressive
ideals of the teacher education movements of the 1970s.
Students were subjected to their enthusiastic, but sometimes
uneducative, experiments. Years later, after a first career as a
secondary teacher, Jane became an education academic. One
day, she happened to come across the original report about
the Disadvantaged Schools Program, a pioneering education
program in her home state of Victoria. As noted in Chapter 1,
this program ran from the 1970s to 1990 and was primarily
designed to address educational inequity (Connell et al.,
1992). Jane happened to glance at the acknowledgments
section, which listed all the participating schools. Her former

secondary school was listed first. Jane's initial reaction was visceral feelings of shock, shame, and denial. These emotional reactions made her realize how deep seated the power of a word such as disadvantage was as a discursive formation, and how it had burrowed deep into her psyche, particularly as a child.

In turn, Jane's reaction to seeing her school named (and "shamed") brought back a key turning point for her in developing a more reflexive consciousness about the stigma of disadvantage that she had absorbed. In her first year of university, she studied sociology. Part of the compulsory readings were those written by sociologist Emile Durkheim, whose deterministic views of the "disadvantaged" portrayed marginalized communities as stuck in an unending cycle of poverty. As Jane read Durkheim's theories, it struck her that he was describing her experiences of the social class from which she had come. Her initial reaction was depression. How could she ever escape this cycle of disadvantage? He was an expert and had described Jane's background and family experiences so accurately. Who was she, a mere first-year university student, to argue with the famous Durkheim?

And then Jane had a lightbulb moment. She was reading about these theories at university—the first in her family to complete high school and go to university. She had got there because of individual merit and new federal government investments to encourage larger numbers of students from low socioeconomic status backgrounds to go to university. This realization helped Jane as a young woman to understand that experts were not gods who should never be questioned and that government policies could be constructive in breaking the shackles of poverty. It helped her understand that there existed other kinds of valued knowledge such as the life experiences of poor family and communities. Finally, it brought home to Jane the attendant risks when privileged forms of knowledge such as sociological theories are used to keep poor people in their "rightful place." Of course, Jane did not have all these revelations at once, but it opened a crack in her worship of the pantheon of experts and led to her critical questioning of "book learning."

Jane's story is not unusual. The prime minister of Australia shares a similar story that has profoundly shaped his life experiences and political trajectory. Many of you may recognize parts of his and Jane's stories and tell something similar with your unique inflections. What Jane experienced in her formative years could be described as a form of "feeling power"—a term coined by the feminist Megan Boler (1999) in her powerful book about the emotions of education. As a new university student reading Durkheim's theory, Jane felt power in Boler's first definition, the power of discourses and privileged knowledge to classify and stereotype whole groups of people as the disadvantaged (Boler, 1999). But she also felt power in Boler's second sense of the phrase—that is, a form of anger that stimulated her to take positive action to reflect, to push back, and to resist. This latter sense of power as resistance profoundly shaped Jane's academic and personal trajectories.

Jane's story also reveals the multidimensional and multifaceted nature of disadvantage. For Jane's mother, the combination of being female, poor, from a non-Anglophone, minority religious background and lacking recognized work skills intersected in ways that compounded her (and her children's) experiences of inequity. As discussed in Chapter 1, reducing Jane's family's experiences of disadvantage to a single-use term obscured the complex ways they experienced and enacted such disadvantage as individuals and collectively. The next section of this chapter therefore explores the origins of intersectionality and why it is so useful as a concept when it comes to unpacking taken-for-granted assumptions that underlie the concept of disadvantage.

Origins of Intersectionality

The African American feminist legal scholar Kimberlé Crenshaw is credited with introducing the concept of intersectionality. In her groundbreaking scholarship, she forensically examined the basis of US antidiscrimination employment laws for Black women who were experiencing work-based inequality and discrimination (Crenshaw, 1989, 1991). She pointed out that this group of workers were forced to choose between taking formal action against employers based on either racial *or* gender discrimination but not on both kinds of discrimination. Yet, it was clear that the discrimination they faced was because they were Black *and* women, for white women did not face similar kinds of racial discrimination in the workplace. Crenshaw (1989) argued Black women's experiences of discrimination were interconnected and could not be compartmentalized into a single axis framework of gender or race. Such a framework distorted their experiences of discrimination and was a "problematic consequence of the tendency to treat race and gender as mutually exclusive categories of experience and analysis" (p. 139).

Although coined as a concept by Crenshaw in 1989, the notion of intersectionality is deeply rooted in the experiences and thinking of women of color from the nineteenth century onwards (Collins & Chepp, 2013). It is grounded in political traditions of "struggles for freedom from multiple systems of oppression and for social justice" (Wilkinson & MacDonald, 2022, p. 91). This historical grounding in resistance and struggle underpins its definition—that is, "as particular forms of intersecting oppressions, for example, intersections of race and gender, or of sexuality and nation. Intersectional paradigms remind us that oppression cannot be reduced to one fundamental type, and that oppressions work together in producing injustice" (Collins, 2000, p. 21).

The concept of intersectionality is also deeply rooted in the thinking, experiences, and political movements of Indigenous and First Nations women in postsettler nations such as Australia, Canada, New Zealand, and the United States and among women from non-Anglophone backgrounds. In Australia, there is a long history of activism and research by Indigenous and non-Anglophone educators who have been systematically examining the intersectional nature of gender, race, class, ethnicity, and, more recently, sexuality and its implications for communities (c.f., Bottomley, 1976; Huggins, 1989; Moreton-Robinson, 2020; Pallotta-Chiarolli, & Rajkhowa, 2017; Tsolidis, 1986). Similar patterns of activism and political and academic contributions can be seen in work undertaken by others in the Global North and South, such as the pioneering research of Indigenous scholars Linda Tuhiwai Smith (1999) and Kumari Jayawardena (1986), to name but a few.

In sum, intersectionality provides a crucial analytic framework for teacher education. It does so by providing a lens through which to understand how specific social categories intersect with other axes of subordination—that is, gender, race, ethnicity, class, and/or sexuality—to reproduce advantages or disadvantages experienced by groups of students. Moreover, as noted in Chapter 1, it assists us in understanding the accumulative impact of discrimination toward students—for example, the adoption of punitive behavior management regimes with Black and Indigenous students and those from vilified minority groups (Milner, 2013). Moreover, thinking about disadvantage with and through an intersectional lens helps us to repudiate the notion of disadvantage as a defining identity, rather than an experience. Jane's personal experiences of being stigmatized and underestimated echo those of many who belong to historically marginalized communities and who have pushed back against disadvantage as a defining identity and discursive formation—that is, "the disadvantaged." In brief, understanding disadvantage through an intersectional lens allows us to address one of the questions raised at the end of Chapter 1—namely, whose purposes does a concept such as disadvantage serve, when, and why? The next sections explore these questions through the lens of one such "vilified minority group" (Milner, 2013, p. xx): students of refugee and asylum-seeking backgrounds who have settled in Australia.

Positioning Students from Refugee and Asylum-Seeking Backgrounds as Disadvantaged in Education

Global forced displacement of populations has increased over the last thirty years. As of mid-2021, 84 million people worldwide were forcibly displaced, the highest figures since the Second World War (UNHCR, 2022b). Forty-two percent of this figure were children below the age of eighteen years. Forcibly displaced children are far less likely to attend or complete school. Current estimates are that 48 percent of all refugee children remain out of school (UNHCR, n.d.). Five percent of refugees are enrolled in tertiary education compared to the global average of non-refugees enrolled in higher education, which stands at 39 percent (UNHCR, 2022a).

Those individuals and families who are eventually settled in host nations may have experienced years of interrupted or, in some cases, no education. They may suffer from ongoing psychological distress due to repeated experiences of trauma. Most will experience a range of other issues including financial precarity, not being fluent in the host nation's language, and so on. The multidimensional nature of disadvantage experienced by students of refugee and asylum-seeking backgrounds has led to ongoing "calls from policy makers … educators … and researchers for fresh ideas and strategies to reduce students' failure and exclusion and assist schools in filling gaps in prior learning" (Kaukko & Wilkinson, 2020, p. 1175).

However, education discourses that focus primarily on students' educational disadvantage—that is, gaps in knowledge and prior learning—run the risk of solidifying these inequities (Kaukko & Wilkinson, 2020). These kinds of deficit discourses underestimate children's capacities, as the prime minister of Australia poignantly observes in the opening quotation to these sections. For children and youth from South Sudan in Australian schools who have refugee backgrounds, the considerable funds of knowledge (Moll et al., 1992) and informal learning capacities that these students bring to their formal education are overlooked (Wilkinson et al., 2017). Instead, discourses of disadvantage "paint a picture of schools as remedial places where both teachers and students struggle in bridging gaps in refugee students' learning" (Kaukko & Wilkinson, 2020, p. 1175). Moreover, as noted in Chapter 1, the labeling of such students as disadvantaged can further cement barriers to their educational achievements (Fuligni, 2007) and is a form of soft bigotry (Dumenden, 2014). This labeling of disadvantage is further compounded for refugee-background students from visible minorities, such as Africa and the Middle East, who are more likely to experience racism and not complete secondary education in Australia (Correa-Velez et al., 2017). Therefore, an emerging body of research aims to disrupt unproblematized assumptions about disadvantage that function to locate these students in their "rightful" place— that is, as "other" to predominantly white Christian student populations (c.f., Dumenden, 2014; Kaukko & Wilkinson, 2021; Major et al., 2013; Naidoo, 2015; Naidoo & Adoniou, 2019; Wilkinson & Lloyd-Zantiotis, 2017).

Implications of Disadvantage When Seen through the Lens of Students of Refugee Backgrounds

There is no doubt that many students of refugee backgrounds experience multiple disadvantages when it comes to education. This is due to factors such as trauma, lack of formal education, poverty, racism, and being members of vilified minorities. These factors can have accumulative and compounding impacts on their social and academic outcomes (Graham et al., 2016).

However, there is a deeper picture here that concepts such as intersectionality helps to surface. For example, one of the problems with terms such as *refugees* and *asylum seekers* is that they can homogenize, essentialize, and paper over the very real differences within and between groups from refugee backgrounds. Like disadvantage, such terms obscure the multidimensional nature of what it means to experience forced displacement and its intersectionality (Severs, 2016). Such language flattens out the complex historical, religious, ethnic, cultural, and linguistic diversities within and between groups. It disguises how multiple axes of gender, "race," and class cut across how forced displacement is variously experienced and enacted. The first point—essentializing groups—is illustrated by the quotation below. It came from a principal of a high school who was taking part in a study of the settlement of South Sudanese refugee background students in regional Australian (Wilkinson & Langat, 2012). He was discussing how to raise teachers' awareness of a new student demographic in their predominantly monocultural school— that is, South Sudanese students from refugee backgrounds. The principal observed:

> We had to ... discourage people ... from saying things like, the African kids do this or the African kids think this way ... You can't simply lump them all under the one group ... We had quite a number of people from Sudan. Their literacy background will depend very much on which way they got out of the country. If they went through Egypt and were in camps in Egypt then they come from an Arabic background as well as their own Indigenous language or languages. ...

> But, and that was another thing that we had to get the staff to realize ... what it was like in their country and what their experiences were, and also their ... own relationship with their country ... with the colonial background of their country. So there's a whole range of issues.

Yet it is not enough to dismiss terms such as refugees out of hand. There are clear advantages to being legally recognized as a refugee. It allows stakeholders to advocate for change and leverage funding that can make a critical difference to life chances. Individuals who have been legally declared refugees in Australia—after a long and arduous process—are able to access myriad resources such as English language programs, health care, welfare benefits, the right to work, and so on. Schools that have more than a certain number of students of refugee background attract Commonwealth funding to support language programs and specialist staffing. For children and young people of refugee backgrounds, such legal recognition allows them to enroll in Australian Government schools for free. It allows them to access university education and pay fees at a domestic student rate, while deferring payment until and unless they earn above a certain income level.

Moreover, the *educational* consequences of not identifying students who come from refugee backgrounds are very clear. For instance, unlike schools, many Australian universities lack specific policies to identify and support students from refugee backgrounds (Naidoo et al., 2015; Naidoo et al., 2018). Hence, these students struggle to access the kinds of resources and supports that will assist them in achieving academic success (Wilkinson, 2018). They may be marked as "too visible" in the system due to their skin color, language, accents, and so on, but at the same time, they are rendered *invisible* due to these policy silences and lack of extra resourcing (Webb et al., 2021). After struggling to access higher education in host nations, some students may become lost in the system due to myriad barriers and drop out before completing their studies (Harris & Marlowe, 2011; Morrice, 2009; Terry et al., 2016). For students whose claims for asylum have not yet been legally recognized in Australia, access and participation in university education are even more precarious (Dunwoodie et al., 2020).

However, the stigmatizing impact of this kind of labeling is also profound, particularly when such labels confer a form of identity—for example, "refugees," "asylum seekers"—rather than an experience. Such labeling is frequently accompanied in host nations such as Australia with virulent racism in the media and society (Blair et al., 2017). Widespread discrimination is regularly directed at those who have experienced forced displacement and who are seen as "visibly different" from the imaginary "white space" of Australia (Uptin, 2021). Unsurprisingly, many students who have experienced forced displacement may refuse to identify with the term refugee or asylum seeker. They may actively conceal their background experiences from friends and educators (Webb et al., 2021). In a study of refugee-background students transitioning into Australian higher education (Naidoo et al., 2015), one male university graduate from a South Sudanese background made some powerful observations about the felt consequences of such labeling:

> There's a tendency [in Australian universities] of giving African refugees a special consideration. But I find it partly to be dirty and partly discriminatory … [Instead] the universities could establish clear parameters as of how do we grade someone who has backlog in their education system.
>
> (p. 117)

He noted the stigmatizing and disempowering impact of constantly being defined as a "victim":

> The more you keep, from my personal experience, defining me as vulnerable, the more I feel vulnerable … But, the more you challenge me to get out of my vulnerability the better. So my suggestion is how can we challenge them rather than sympathize with them? Because it makes someone—I never like someone who has empathy over me [laughs].
>
> (p. 117)

Indeed, research suggests that educational achievement for students in schools and higher education who have experienced forced displacement are less dependent on their previous educational experiences. Rather, they are more dependent on the levels of aspiration educators hold for them, combined with appropriate academic and emotional supports to help them engage with the system (Brownlees & Finch, 2010; Naidoo et al., 2018).

Conclusion: Usefulness of Intersectionality in Dialogue with Disadvantage

The above examples suggest the following question: Is it that students of refugee backgrounds are disadvantaged, or is it the sociopolitical conditions that have put them in the place of disadvantage? (see also Chapter 1). Two responses to this question arise from more recent research into the educational achievements of students of refugee backgrounds. First, rather than homogenizing these students as a disadvantaged group, there needs to be a thoughtful understanding of the immensely varied sociopolitical conditions that may have led to a place of disadvantage. Second, rather than using this understanding to paint such students as deficit and lacking in educational capability, an intersectional lens can help us to understand the crucial strengths, informal learning practices, and funds of knowledge that many bring to their education (Kaukko & Wilkinson, 2020; Santoro & Wilkinson, 2015; Wilkinson et al., 2017). For instance, some students may not have had the more seamless formal education experiences of other students but bring a rich oral culture that educators can draw on in highly productive ways—for example, through storycrafting (Kaukko, 2021).

To summarize, to be labeled as a refugee and therefore disadvantaged is a discursive construction that carries judgmental overtones of pity and a sense of superiority as settler nations assert their dominance over those who are the recipients of their largesse (Uptin, 2021). Furthermore, the toxic refugee policies of decades of Australian governments have led to major increases in racist vilification and attacks that have resulted in racist and discriminatory attitudes (Blair et al., 2017). The accumulative impact of such racism leads to educational disengagement and underachievement for students of refugee background, particularly those from visible minorities in predominantly white settler nations such as Australia (Correa-Velez et al., 2017).

However, understanding what it means to experience disadvantage through an intersectional lens and using the language associated with it in more critical ways can begin to break down these stereotypes. It can begin to open possibilities for a more constructive and productive educational engagement with students, their families, and communities. Chapter 3 explores how a critical approach is necessary in teacher education to prepare teachers with a deep, intersectional, and nuanced understanding of disadvantage.

CHAPTER THREE

What Do Teachers Learn about Disadvantage?

Introduction

Globally, teacher graduate standards or attributes provide sanctioned imperatives around what beginning teachers are supposed to know and do. As Elton-Chalcraft et al. (2017) state, teacher professional standards are policy documents that represent the values of the nation-state. They are, as much as anything else, documents that provide boundaries around the complexities of teaching and are primarily aimed at quantifying, measuring, and standardizing teachers' work (Clarke & Moore, 2013; Mockler, 2022). The presence or absence of equity-related skills, knowledge about the effects of disadvantage, or the social justice dispositions expected of new teachers is symbolic of how any nation defines the work of an effective teacher. They are a public statement on what constitutes quality teaching. Consequently, graduate teacher standards have significant influence not only on how teachers perceive and understand disadvantage, but also on how important they believe addressing equity (and redressing disadvantage) is to the profession.

Although the word disadvantage may never explicitly appear in teacher graduate standards, overall, most do include

TABLE 1 *Disadvantage in teacher professional standards.*

Country	Direct extracts from the standards	Description
South Africa South African Council for Educators (SACE) Professional Teaching Standards (2020)	"The South African education system is hampered by persistent inequality, high learner drop-out rates, and variable teaching quality. Thus, there is a need to develop a common understanding of professional teaching practice." 1.3 Teachers respect different aspects of learners' identities (including gender, race, language, culture, sexual orientation, and dis/ability), and believe that these diversities can be a strength and resource for teaching and learning. 3.0 Teachers support social justice and the redress of inequalities within their educational institutions and society more broadly. 3.2. Teachers have a responsibility to identify and challenge policies and practices that discriminate against, marginalize, or exclude learners.	This is an example of an explicit reference to inequality, social justice, or disadvantage in professional teacher standards. Furthermore, Standard 3.2 is an example of an explicit set of standards in identifying the political nature of teachers' work to influence or challenge policy and to redress inequalities within society or beyond school walls.
Sierra Leone Teaching Service Commission Professional Standards for Teachers and School Leaders in Sierra Leone (2017)	STANDARD 5: Know physical, socio-cultural, and psychological characteristics of learners 5.1 Diversity among learners, e.g., gender, language, urban-rural, economic and social background Demonstrate knowledge and understanding of the diversity among learners with respect to the physical, socio-cultural, and psychological backgrounds of students STANDARD 12: Safeguard human rights and lives	These standards are representative in framing teachers' work through a physical, sociocultural, and psychological lens. The standards do, however, also define teachers' work as related to human rights and the rights of the child.

Republic of Ireland Teaching Council Code of Professional Conduct for Teachers (2nd ed., 2016)	12.1 Design and implement practices to guarantee the fundamental rights of the child which shall include those found in the following: the Convention on the Rights of the Child, the African Charter on the Rights and Welfare of the Child, the Child Rights Act, and other human rights instruments such as CEDAW (Convention on the elimination of all forms of discrimination against women), the Convention on the Rights of Persons with Disabilities, and the right to education in emergencies.
	
	Core value: "RESPECT
	    Teachers uphold human dignity and promote equality and emotional and cognitive development. In their professional practice, teachers demonstrate respect for spiritual and cultural values, diversity, social justice, freedom, democracy and the environment."
	    Teachers should:
	    1.3 be committed to equality and inclusion and to respecting and accommodating diversity including those differences arising from gender, civil status, family status, sexual orientation, religion, age, disability, race, ethnicity, membership of the Traveler community and socio-economic status, and any further grounds as may be referenced in equality legislation in the future
		Like the other examples, teachers are required to understand and teach to difference. These standards include the environment, religious freedom, and a specific reference to the traveler community as a direct reference to one of the most disadvantaged communities in Ireland and throughout Europe.

statements that require new teachers to teach everyone equally, create safe and equitable classrooms, know their students' backgrounds, and communicate in culturally appropriate ways. While the specifics may vary from country to country, three examples of reference to disadvantage in teacher professional standards from both the Global North and the Global South provide some scope for comparison and may allow readers of this book to consider how the graduate teacher standards in their own countries are written.

A Brief Critique of Graduate Teacher Standards

As discussed, policy documents such as teacher professional standards represent the values of the nation-state, and as such, they carry weight not just in determining what new teachers must be able to demonstrate, but also in signposting what school systems purport to value. Many nations have developed graduate teacher standards that regulate, in varying degrees of detail, what graduate teachers should know, believe, and enact in their teaching. At this point in time, at least some of these graduate standards refer to providing equitable and inclusive teaching related to addressing inequity or disadvantage.

In Australia, the Australian Institute for Teaching and School Leadership (AITSL, 2018) produces the Australian Professional Standards for Teachers which were most recently revised in 2018. There are several clauses in the Standards that refer to culturally responsive teaching, including one clause on reconciliation between Indigenous and non-Indigenous peoples. There is also a clause about being "responsive to the learning strengths and needs of students from diverse linguistic, cultural, religious and socioeconomic backgrounds." While the word disadvantage is used only indirectly, a general ethos of the Standards relates to redressing disadvantage and to requiring teachers to demonstrate principles of equity and equitable practice.

Graduate teacher standards represent changing political landscapes, are highly political, and are often contested. For instance, at the time of writing, Australian Professional Standards for Teachers 1.4., *Strategies for teaching Aboriginal and Torres Strait Islander students*, requires graduate teachers to demonstrate broad knowledge and understanding of the impact of culture, cultural identity, and linguistic background on the education of students from Aboriginal and Torres Strait Islander backgrounds. APST 2.4 (Understand and respect Aboriginal and Torres Strait Islander people to promote reconciliation between Indigenous and non-Indigenous Australians) requires graduate teachers to demonstrate broad knowledge and understanding of and respect for Aboriginal and Torres Strait Islander histories, cultures, and languages. These standards reflect the cross-curriculum priority set by the Australian Curriculum, Assessment and Reporting Authority that the national school curriculum will provide all young Australians with a deeper understanding and appreciation of Aboriginal and Torres Strait Islander histories and cultures, knowledge traditions, and holistic world views. Although some critics, such as Thorpe et al. (2021), feel these statements are still too weak, too difficult to implement, and merely an add-on, the mandatory inclusion of Indigenous curriculum, as well as statements about how Indigenous studies (and Indigenous students) are to be taught, is an important statement to include in the graduate teacher standards. But the inclusion of Aboriginal and Torres Strait Islander curriculum and approaches in the APSTs are at risk because in Australia, as in other parts of the world, there are vocal and powerful lobbies who feel teaching has become too "political," biased, and dominated by "the left." If the Australian Curriculum is revised, as is happening in other hegemonically white-dominated nations, to elevate the study of Western and Christian heritage, the APSTs would also be revised. In other words, what and how preservice teachers are taught about equity, social change, or the effects of disadvantage are highly contingent and precarious and "fraught with cultural and political tensions" (Salter & Maxwell, 2016, p. 296).

While many are pleased to see teachers required to graduate with knowledge seemingly related to equity, others remain concerned about its superficiality. In what is required by quality teachers in nations such as the United States, Canada, Australia, New Zealand, and much of Europe (Santoro & Kennedy, 2016), culturally responsive pedagogies are often named in professional standards. However, Moodie and Patrick (2017) call for teacher educators to "disrupt some of the more problematic interpretations of the Standards" (p. 443), claiming such general things as requiring teachers to demonstrate "cultural sensitivity" and "respect" as the solution to educational disparity serves simply "to reinvent the settler grammars" (p. 451). Santoro and Kennedy (2016) concur, stating "simply knowing that students do not all share the same cultural and linguistic backgrounds is not sufficient" (p. 214). They point out the silences and omissions in the use of euphemistic language that makes injustice and inequity invisible, claiming that the language of teacher professional standards, such as referring to "students with varying backgrounds" and repeatedly using the common language of "diversity" is too generic. For instance, talking generically about diversity can be perceived as a refusal to name exactly which groups (Indigenous peoples, people with disabilities, single mothers, elderly women, and racialized individuals) have been historically oppressed and marginalized. Santoro and Kennedy (2016) suggest this "raises questions about the inherently political nature of professional standards as being reflective of wider social policy priorities within individual nation states, thus illustrating the power of the standards documents to 'produce the subject' rather than simply reflect it" (p. 218).

These debates take place in many nations. According to Thompson and Menter (2017), in England, there is no direct or explicit mention of disadvantage in the Teachers' Standards, but it is implied that teachers need to be aware of the social, cultural, and economic environments of the schools and communities in which their students live and learn (p. 4). This awareness, or even "empathy" (as explicitly referred to in the APSTs; Victorian Institute of Teaching, 2010), is the baseline goal for most graduate teacher standards that focus on sensitivity training but not ways to become active change-makers or activists. Cultural awareness comes from a longstanding tradition of social justice education but can be stuck in a cycle of care, unable to change the oppressive systems that perpetuate the disadvantage in the first place. Muniz's (2019) survey of cultural responsiveness in teaching standards in fifty states in the United States observed, "Some teaching standards stand out for their tremendous depth and nuance, while others are broad and vague in their approach" (p. 22).

Graduate teacher standards regulate what teachers should know, as well as guiding what teacher educators should teach and on what basis they assess their preservice teachers. In the following sections we provide brief critical comments on two programs that have influenced teacher education with respect to understanding disadvantage. One is the Teach for All model, which purports to develop collective leadership to improve education and expand opportunity for all children, so they can shape a better future for themselves and the world around them." The other is Ruby Payne's Poverty Framework, which has gained traction as a popular professional development program for teachers to understand their students who live in poverty.

Teach for All

Teach for All was co-founded by Wendy Kopp (former CEO of Teach for America), and while it is referred to as a "global community of leaders," it functions as an alternative teacher preparation program. Teach for All serves as a conglomerate for sixty-one partner programs and initiatives worldwide, funded as not-for-profits privately (through philanthropic trust funds, individuals, and corporations). The "teach for" programs primarily retrain degree-holding applicants to teach in underserved communities, in some cases bypassing the regulatory structures of traditional institutions for teacher preparation and supervision. These preparatory programs are often short "blocks" or intensives spanning around six weeks and are attached to two-year contracts with schools. In the context of educational crises of inequity, teacher shortages, and in the name of addressing this inequity, Teach for All is a well-known employment-based system, whereby teachers, mostly career changers, are fast-tracked to historically hard-to-staff disadvantaged or low socioeconomic schools.

The teach-for programs are premised on addressing teacher shortages in disadvantaged schools by attracting untapped, high-quality career changers to become teachers and consider pathways as educational leaders. A belief in meritocracy underpins the program in its underlying belief that attracting the "best and brightest" into the teaching profession and placing them in "underprivileged" schools will bring parity to the school system, equalizing opportunities for young people who would not otherwise be exposed to the best teachers (Crawford-Garrett et al., 2021). While the "teach for" programs focus on addressing inequity and disadvantage, numerous studies have noted that corps members generally "focus on test-based accountability despite engagement with sociocultural science education scholarship" (McNew-Birren et al., 2017, p. 460). In other words, teachers are considered successful if they improve schools' rankings or test scores. This illustrates a particularly neoliberal approach to understanding how equality can be measured. Nevertheless, it should be noted that measuring teachers' success by their students' academic outcomes is not limited to the goals of "teach for." Concerns about which kinds of evidence count for teachers to prove they "make a difference" are expressed across the board.

While the "teach for" programs may attract quality career changers to apply, they are less successful at producing quality teachers who will stay in the profession (Crawford-Garrett, Oldham & Thomas, 2021), However, the claim is that these "best and brightest" graduates will understand equity issues and are considered equally successful if they do not stay in the teaching profession but ultimately take up educational leadership or senior policy positions. While "teach for" programs generally need a university affiliate for teacher accreditation, there are concerns about the long-term impact of a not-for-profit organization like Teach for All competing with university degree-granting initial teacher education programs. These represent broader concerns about the privatization of initial teacher education (Thomas et al., 2021). Some criticisms of the "teach for" programs are that they (1) undermine tertiary initial teacher education programs by claiming a teacher only needs six weeks or so of preparation before they are qualified enough to teach their own classes without supervision (Kretchmar et al., 2018; Rowan et al., 2014), (2) undermine and take jobs away from university-prepared or experienced teachers, and (3) reinforce the flawed idea that teaching can only be learned "on the job." For instance, there is never a guarantee of the quality of their mentors or that what "teach for" participants encounter in schools is good practice. Additionally, some teach-for program participants recount the "shock" of being "dropped into a complex school before they felt ready or without proper support" (Brewer, 2014; Lefebvre & Thomas, 2017). Another criticism is that the "teach for" programs are missionary in their zeal, mostly attracting white, middle-class professionals to teach as "corps members" in disadvantaged schools in order to help or save children and families from backgrounds very unlike their own (Thomas, 2018).

Nonetheless, the "teach for" programs are well supported, well resourced, and favored by some governments and schools who see them as able to address the increasingly crisis-level teacher shortages in a short, escalated period. They are clearly a "growing and important source of teachers in low-income schools" (Chiang et al., 2017) and will increasingly be so in the post-pandemic world where teacher shortages are internationally at crisis level.

In the next section, we discuss an equally controversial professional development program, Ruby Payne's Poverty Framework.

Ruby Payne's Poverty Framework

Ruby Payne's framework for understanding poverty was first (self-) published in the United States in 2001. Now in its sixth edition, it accompanies workshops, workbooks, and resources targeted at school teachers and school administrators in order for them to understand, build relationships with, and help their students from backgrounds of poverty. Payne delivers these tools via her for-profit business named Aha! Process, Inc. The approach aims to prepare teachers to work with students in poverty through re-educating students in the "culture" of the middle class (something Payne believes young people in poverty lack). The message has been well, if uncritically, received by schools. Using Payne's strategies, students and families in poverty can be understood as depicted through checkboxes and lists that describe them. While Payne explains that people in poverty do not always understand the "hidden rules" of schooling, poor people have their own hidden rules that teachers must understand—such as, for poor people from generational poverty, people are possessions: "It is worse to steal someone's girlfriend than a thing" or if you are poor, you "laugh when you are disciplined; it is a way to save face" (Payne, n.d.). Generalized, essentialized, and stereotyped claims such as these have brought Payne under serious criticism despite her book and resources having sold over 1.8 million copies. Many critics of Payne's framework insist teachers must resist simplified explanations of "high-poverty communities" such as those offered in Payne's *A Framework for Understanding Poverty* and *Bridges out of Poverty* (2018), which have become popular for professional development even in Australia.

Many scholars have critiqued Payne's premise, which is that middle-class teachers can learn to understand how "poor people" think, act, and feel. Bomer et al. (2008) are critical of Payne's framework, using it as an example of a deficit perspective that draws on an unproven and discredited notion of a "culture of poverty," something Payne is accredited with having both hypothesized and popularized. Others have identified the framework as victim blaming and paternalistic (i.e., hypothesizing that poor people just do not know better and can be "fixed"; Kane, 2019). Others are concerned that the stereotypes Payne propagates end up blaming the poor. This is a challenge for teachers who are instructed to "know their community" but are cautioned against deficit thinking and stereotyping. While Payne has more recently added chapters to unpack such things as race and immigration, this was to address criticisms that intersectional understandings seemed so absent from the original framework (Thomas, 2010).

Another criticism of the Poverty Framework is its slick production as a product that "peddles poverty for profit" (Gorski, 2008), something Koksvik and Øverland (2019) consider unethical and "morally illicit" (p. 341).

Critical Perspectives on Disadvantage: What Should Teachers Know?

Despite the challenges and concerns that policy and some popular approaches to addressing disadvantage through teacher education may raise, their influence leaves a mark on how both teacher educators and preservice teachers perceive and understand disadvantage. Logically, if what teachers learn about disadvantage will have an impact on their future careers, this could be an opportunity for them to become agents of change. It seems essential, then, to engage teachers in a critical dialogue about disadvantage, considering its intersectionality and operating under a paradigm of possibility to open a new way of preparing future teachers (Howard, 2010). This includes taking a stance to challenge injustice, reflecting on how to eradicate discrimination, and educating preservice teachers to end exclusion of those students who have experienced systematic marginalization.

According to Cochran-Smith et al. (2016), for teachers to provide a high-quality education to all students from marginalized groups, they must pay attention to the existing conditions that perpetuate educational and social inequalities, which might have remained invisible for many teachers during their preparation programs. To do so, teachers need to engage in dialogue with those people who have been systematically marginalized to know and understand their students' lifeworlds—that is, the "reservoir of taken-for-granteds, of unshaken convictions that participants in communication draw upon in cooperative processes of interpretation" (Habermas, 1987, p. 124). This occurs in dialogic spaces where teachers can listen to students' and families' voices in an egalitarian dialogue. Indeed, research has shown the power of dialogic practices in high-poverty schools to create affordances for newly arrived teachers to take a critical stance against disadvantage and to become agents of transformation (García-Carrión et al., 2020).

Indeed, teachers' ability to engage with students and support their educational and social success is shaped by what teachers know about their students' lives, family backgrounds, and learning needs, as well as by their pedagogical knowledge (Carter & Darling-Hammond, 2016). However, this might create a tension between learning about the reality of those students who experience disadvantage and generating deficit discourses that legitimize the stereotypes against those historically marginalized. According to Darling-Hammond (2016), a culture of poverty still exists that situates achievement disparities in the presumably deficient homes and communities of students who are erroneously believed to consider education and academic achievement unimportant. This deficit view has affected many groups of students who have experienced exclusion and stigmatization through multiple systems of oppression (see Chapter 2), including race, ethnicity, class, gender, or sexuality. Among those, the case of the Roma people in the European landscape shows how for centuries they have been trapped in a vicious circle of isolation, poverty, unemployment, and poor education (European Commission, 2019) and have suffered from the common belief among many teachers they "have a natural disaffection for education and for schools" (Gómez & Vargas, 2003, p. 559). As with many other cultural groups worldwide, they have suffered the pervasive "deficit thinking" (Valencia, 2010), which situates the problem of school failure and exclusion within students, families, and communities and reinforces the idea that disadvantage is an individual trait or a social or cultural identity (García & Guerra, 2004).

Therefore, from a critical perspective on disadvantage, it is urgently still needed for teachers to dismantle deficit thinking (Valencia, 2010). Although there is a substantial body of scholarship, which has been essential to shifting perspectives from a deficit-based approach to one of valuing the language, literacy, and cultural practices of historically vulnerable students (Ladson-Billings, 1994; López, 2016; Moll et al., 1992), it is also important to know and reconsider how the disadvantage is understood. Understanding disadvantage as historical and contextual seems essential for teachers to counteract traditions of low expectations for those systematically marginalized who have been blamed and labeled for the detrimental impact of contextual and historical conditions. Building a shared understanding and a common language, something which has been pointed out as being particularly important in teacher education pedagogies (Grossman & Dean, 2019; Peercy et al., 2022), can also offer affordances for teachers and teacher educators to collectively rethink their understanding of the term disadvantage as contextual and, consequently, learn to act against inequities in education.

From this perspective, teachers can challenge social injustice by taking seriously the intersectionality of disadvantage to "create institutions and knowledge that build more powerful and transformative collective identities" (Apple, 2013, p. 20). Therefore, and aligned with critical pedagogy, teachers should be prepared to act with a language of possibility (Freire & Macedo, 1987). A language of possibility will enable teachers to empower students to make sense of their own histories, life experiences, and cultures, while gaining knowledge and tools of the dominant culture to overcome the inequities they have suffered (Freire & Macedo, 1987; Macedo, 1994). Hence, teachers and students make sense of the historical conditions of disadvantage, but they embrace a history as a possibility, never as predetermined (Freire, 2000). As in Freire's (1997) theory, critical perspectives on disadvantage call for the possibilities inherent in transformation since "we are transformative beings and not beings for accommodation" (p. 36). Taking a transformative stance when thinking about disadvantage does not mean a naïve view of the reality. That would risk ignoring the existent and persistent inequalities many minority groups still suffer. According to Freire (2004), transformation is "not a matter of idealism. Imagination and conjecture about a different world, than the one of oppression, are necessary to the praxis of historical 'subjects' (agents) in the process of transforming reality" (p. 30). Teachers need to know about the historical and contextual factors that produce disadvantage and about the possibilities of transforming those realities, because teaching is not culturally neutral; it is political, contextually specific, and powerful enough to engage or disaffect students (Carter & Darling-Hammond, 2016). However, such a language of possibility cannot be learned only through discourse in teacher education programs but through a combination of reflection and action, following Freire's (2000) notion of praxis, as discussed in Chapter 5.

In initial teacher education, a community-engaged framework (Lampert, 2020) shows its potential for future teachers to engage teachers effectively with those communities who have suffered from disadvantage. Within this framework, preservice teachers participate in programs with community perspectives embedded in their curriculum, but they are also involved with local families throughout their programs. They learn with the community and respect their local and contextual differences, incorporating what they learn into their work through a language of possibility. Indeed, a decisive aspect that has been pointed out in community-engaged teacher preparation programs (Zeichner et al., 2016; Zygmunt et al., 2022) is valuing and privileging students' and families' funds of knowledge (Moll et al., 1992). From this perspective, community-engaged teacher preparation differs from any other community-based initiative, where teachers are simply physically based in a community (Zygmunt et al., 2022). It implies that teachers authentically learn from such privileged insights that students, families, and communities offer as part of the historically and culturally accumulated bodies of knowledge and skills that enhance their ability to survive and thrive (Moll et al., 1992, p. 133).

Preservice teachers can access students' and families' funds of knowledge during professional experience placements when classrooms and schools create dialogic spaces for valuing and elevating such knowledge. For example, in some programs in Spain, Brazil, and Mexico, among other countries, historically marginalized students participate in dialogic literary gatherings where they share their opinions and reflect on their own histories and experiences by discussing literary texts (Santiago-Garabieta et al., 2021). In these dialogic encounters, students' and families' knowledge is valued and shared in an egalitarian dialogue with teachers; it is a space for collective meaning-making and for understanding people as agents of social change (Soler, 2015). This creates affordances for future teachers to know about disadvantage through the voices of the people who have experienced it for themselves in a space that traditionally has not included them, such as Roma girls, children with disabilities, boys in rural areas, among others. With these educational strategies and pedagogical practices, teachers can foster a collective understanding to challenge prejudices and lead to transformative learning to ultimately benefit those students, families, and communities ultimately disadvantaged by the educational effects of disadvantage itself.

Traditionally the knowledge that has been valued and recognized in teacher education programs is situated at the university or at the school—that is, "within the system"— whereas the knowledge of historically marginalized communities is typically perceived as less relevant and devalued. Often, teacher preparation programs do not include the narratives of those funds of knowledge (Zygmunt et al., 2022). Consequently, it is unlikely that future teachers will be prepared to capitalize on students' and families' funds of knowledge to work effectively in the classroom. Some pathways to close that gap refer to building partnerships across institutional boundaries, expanding the walls of the university to incorporate people and other institutions previously absent, such as associations or community movements, and forging new relationships between preservice teachers and the very people who have experienced the effects of disadvantage.

The practice of public narrative (Ganz, 2009) can mobilize teachers and communities in a joint activity through telling, listening, and reflecting on what people who have been traditionally silenced have to say. Public narrative brings together three stories: "the story of self," which communicates a personal story and the values of the person, "the story of us," which is a collective story that shows the shared purpose, goals, and vision, and "the story of now," which is the challenge the community faces and the hope to which they all together can aspire. Preservice teachers can benefit from accessing, valuing, and privileging students' and communities' funds of knowledge, incorporating them into their classrooms or universities. By creating optimal conditions for critical reflection and action, teacher education programs can contribute to the preparation of a critical teaching force ready to tackle the issue of disadvantage from a critical perspective. This will ultimately provide teachers with an alternative discourse that ends deficit thinking and prepares them to act with an ethics of care, love, and solidarity, aiming to transform education as a pathway to transform society.

Conclusion

These are by no means the only ways initial teacher education addresses disadvantage. This chapter aimed to provide a critical snapshot of some of the prevailing and popular approaches that position preservice teachers to learn about disadvantage and that appear strongly influential throughout a teacher's working life.

CHAPTER FOUR

Interviews from Inside Disadvantage

Lived Experience

Prioritizing the opinions of people who have themselves experienced disadvantage is grounded in a concept we consider crucial in preparing equity-minded or democratic teachers. This idea, seemingly obvious, is that no conversations *about* disadvantage should ever take place without the voices and firsthand knowledge of people from that group. This includes classroom or staffroom conversations about why or how disadvantage should be addressed. For instance, there should be fewer (or no) behind-the-door meetings about "what to do about" Indigenous kids, young people with disabilities, LGBTQIA+ kids, or families from any cultural or religious group without representation from those groups.

Teachers should be prepared to teach students from all backgrounds, by listening closely and without preconceived judgment to the most vulnerable families' lived experiences, embracing their experiences as a valid form of knowledge, and prioritizing the voices of people who have so regularly been misrepresented and marginalized. When teachers, who often have very limited engagement with families unlike their own, are informed by peoples' lived experiences it makes prejudice, stereotyping, and Othering less likely (Conus & Fahrni, 2019) and addresses a fear of the unknown that is often cited as an explanation for resistance to inclusive education (Robinson & Goodey, 2018).

Community voices, especially the perspectives of historically vulnerable high-poverty communities, are often inaudible in decisions about how teachers are prepared (Lampert, 2020). However, preservice teachers who *do* receive the opportunity to hear the firsthand experiences and opinions of students, parents, and community members almost unanimously talk about its profound impact (Koch, 2020). Furthermore, living by the rule that nothing must be done without the prioritized input of those most affected is an act of solidarity, leading teachers toward a more critically conscious understanding (Freire, 1973; Yarbrough, 2020) and is imperative for teachers to engage in transformative pedagogical practices (Luguetti & Oliver, 2019).

Listening deeply to lived experiences of disadvantage is of particular importance to preservice teachers. As Zygmunt et al. (2022) explain,

> Awash in social messages that affirm their own values and experiences, white, monolingual educators often view students and families of linguistic, racial, and socioeconomic backgrounds different from their own through a cultural deficit lens. Many schools, both urban and rural, remain racially and economically segregated; and many of those responsible for teaching students neither live in the communities where they teach nor possess knowledge of students' lived experience outside school.
>
> (para. 6)

If teachers are to practice solidarity, we can only address injustice external and internal to education systems with proper representation. In other words, those most affected, young people and their families, must be at the center of teachers' knowledge.

Overall, the aim of this chapter is to present the voices of those who have regularly been invisible or silenced and to accept people as experts in their own experience (Gorski, 2016).

Firsthand Experiences of Disadvantage

In their teacher education programs, preservice teachers are regularly required to take subjects on cultural diversity, inclusive education, or other topics covering pedagogical strategies for supporting students who are historically disadvantaged. Often, they are asked to write assignments on topics such as inclusion or prepare lesson plans for groups of young people perceived as having special needs or circumstances. Yet, it is rare for preservice teachers to hear how young people from disadvantage experience schooling from their personal standpoints.

In reality, there is a bounty of research relying on interviews where the perspectives of children who experience disadvantage are recorded. There is also plenty of research where adults who grew up with disadvantage are asked to reflect on how school felt for them when they were young. These are important firsthand accounts that could more often be included in teacher education. While there is only room here to mention a few of these sources of firsthand accounts, we can give some examples to illustrate their significance to teacher education.

Young People Telling Their Own Stories

Many research projects try to capture the experiences of young people in and out of school. Interviewing is, of course, the most common qualitative research. Ethically designed research with young people recognizes how important it is to hear peoples' own stories, treating their words with respect and providing cultural safety and care.

Just a very few examples are offered here of the insights that can be gained from asking preservice teachers to read and reflect on interview data where young peoples' voices are included. As one example, Boddy's (2019) research includes narratives from young people in care. These recorded stories are from children talking about their families in both challenging and loving ways. Stories like these keep teachers accountable and are important reminders that young people love their families, and their families love them, even though to outsiders (such as seemingly objective teachers), they may seem difficult or dysfunctional. It is harder for preservice teachers to jump to stereotyped or deficit assumptions when they are asked to listen deeply to real experiences. For instance, in Simmons-Horton's (2020) research involving interviews with children in care, one young person very clearly recounted, "My idea of living ... was being home with my family. Being able to go places with my family" (p. 593). Even that one small excerpt from a personal standpoint complicates narratives of good families/bad families that sometimes permeate teachers' beliefs and can lead to a deepened awareness of the trauma of being removed from a family or of having one's family judged.

Very little counteracts deficit stereotypes as much as hearing lived experiences. Bakali's (2016) interviews with Canadian Muslim teenagers offer firsthand accounts of racism that may not be visible to teachers who only see their students in class. In El Ashmawi's (2016) testimonios, American Muslim families tell honest stories of what school is like for them and their children. These include both positive and negative experiences, including encounters with Islamophobia, and in Smith and Hope's (2020) study, young Black American men narrate their own experiences with racism. There are abundant examples including student voice that can be drawn on.

Similarly, Lewis et al.'s (2020) study of sixty-seven LGBTQI+ autistic young people offers the firsthand experiences of teenagers who are "doubly minoritized." These nuanced stories from vulnerable youth can most certainly open the eyes of teachers who can very easily "miss" what is going on for young people, especially the compounded, cumulative nature of intersecting disadvantages.

The stories told in the Australian Life Chances longitudinal study (Taylor, 2014) are yet another example of how young people's own words could be helpful in preparing more equity-minded teachers. This longitudinal study of young people in Melbourne all born in 1990 does not just demonstrate the differences between the experiences of middle-class kids and young people who live with disadvantage, but also counteracts stereotypes by presenting the thoughtful, reflective voices of youth. Hall's (2000) UK study of nine poor, white sixth-, seventh-, and eighth-grade "Canal Street" girls is another example of an ethnographic study that records the stories of young people. In this case, although the stories do not gloss over the experiences of urban adolescent girls who come from painful, traumatic, and violent family backgrounds, they are also stories of significant hope as the girls imagine futures for themselves as strong, independent women. Ethnographies can provide preservice teachers with contextual understandings of difficult realities and can also remind them to channel and facilitate hope.

Qualitative research where interviews with young people or their families have been conducted are useful, but it is important to remember that these are still curated stories, selected by researchers as examples and analyzed by them to illustrate particular points. Nevertheless, these excerpts from interviews, especially from ethnographic studies, provide "lived experiences" to an extent. A concerted effort in teacher education to include readings that embed young people's own words offers rich opportunity for critical reflection.

Adults Speaking Out: Life Stories, Memoirs, Counternarratives, and Testimonio

Above, we advocated for young people's lived experiences to more regularly inform how teachers understand disadvantage. There are also many available and useful texts, including memoirs and autobiographies, where adult writers reflect on their memories of schooling in relation to growing up in poverty or violence, experiencing racism, or encountering exclusion because of disadvantage. These memoirs can take numerous forms but are often motivated by the author's desire to change the experiences for others who may now be in the same situation. Many of these texts are politically motivated, some activist in intent. While some writers may also write in the desire to "heal personal wounds" (Lockhart, 2019), a common reason to write about ones' own experiences with disadvantage is to make sure change occurs and that experiences of disadvantage, often perpetrated by unjust systems (such as school systems), are not experienced by others in the future. Personal stories may be in the form of testimonios (usually firsthand witness accounts from a person, such as a poor woman of color, who has come from the margins of society and tells a story that has been historically silenced) or may offer a counternarrative, such as an alternative version of a commonly held story. An example of a memoir is Tara Westover's (2018) autobiography *Educated* in which she writes about overcoming her violent childhood in a survivalist family in the United States. Westover uses her traumatic childhood as a vehicle for reform and has subsequently written on the inequalities she knows firsthand to be apparent in the United States, including in its school system (Westover, 2019). There are too many memoirs of this sort to note in this chapter, and there are more each year. All these forms of storying—autobiography, memoir, testimonio—allow people to tell their own stories about experiencing (which may or may not include overcoming) difficult or challenging experiences. And perhaps because almost everyone spends their formative lives in school, there are many examples of memoirs, autobiographies, and auto-ethnographies that focus on childhood, youth, and schooling from people who have experienced disadvantage. When published, these life stories with their added self-reflective insights are valuable sources of knowledge for educators.

Memoirs can be a rich source of personal stories, but they need to be used in teacher education with some caution, since popular books can tell good yarns, but they can also be sensationalized or open to misinterpretation once out in the world. Educators who are teaching preservice teachers about disadvantage should be very careful to avoid or decontextualize uncritically considered uses of lived experience stories that can become mere voyeurism, elicit pity responses (Corrigan, 2017), or lead to generalizations. Lived experiences should only be presented if the carefully planned intent is for social change and can, unless used carefully, do more harm than good. The use of lived experiences to inform preservice teachers requires critical and careful understanding, particularly from teacher educators who do not have these lived experiences themselves. For instance, it can be the case that so-called disadvantaged communities are more conservative, authoritarian or stricter with their own children than the policies of the schools in which their children are taught. This is a conundrum teacher educator should be prepared to take on. A "poverty aware teacher education program" (Steinberg & Kruger-Nevo, 2022) requires preservice teachers to reserve judgment and to more consciously learn about the sometimes challenging and varied perspectives of the communities in which they teach.

Nevertheless, with that caveat, the power of personal story seems indisputable. University lectures on disadvantage can influence what preservice teachers know or think, and the evidence is that many teachers enter the profession with entrenched views, such as believing parents from poor families are somehow the cause of their own misfortune. The evidence is also that these views are extremely resistant to change (Lampert & Browne, 2022). A case study at the University of Oxford found that an alarming 40 percent of preservice teachers in a social justice teacher education program held the same views about children in poverty at the end of a specific course in social justice as they had prior to listening to the carefully designed, provocative lectures about economic and social disparities they participated in as part of their course. Despite these students successfully completing assignments on inequity and social justice, their views changed very little from start to end of the social justice curriculum (Ellis et al., 2016). The one thing that did seem to make the most difference were stories from "real" people. One conclusion from the Oxford case study was a conclusion also reached by Thompson (2017), that "entrenched views are hard to change without direct participation of students from impoverished backgrounds and teachers with experience of working to alleviate the effects of poverty for these youngsters" (p. 37). Similarly, a study in Israel, where preservice teachers were exposed to life stories of people in poverty, concluded that the reflexive reading of such life stories can challenge stereotypes, deepen teachers' understanding, and help sensitize them to school pedagogies and practices that exacerbate inequality (Steinberg & Krumer-Nevo, 2022).

Using first-person narratives also ensures that people are able to tell the stories they wish to about themselves, and this aids in controlling the stories others (such as teachers) tell about them. Like using the stories of young people, prioritizing what adults who have experienced disadvantage in their lives say and write allows us to reflect on questions about "whose voices count" (Moodie et al., 2021, p. 6) and to take the perspectives of those who have in fact experienced disadvantage seriously.

Lived Experience of Disadvantage in the Australian Context[1]

In the research that informs this section of the chapter, Lampert invited adults in Australia who self-identified as "disadvantaged" to tell us how they felt about having grown up with the label.

Spectators and Participants

To lead us into these firsthand perspectives, we begin with just two statements from preservice teachers talking *about* disadvantage in order to compare these with statements from people who identify *as having come from* or *lived with the label of* disadvantage. This highlights some of the differences between what Kemmis (2012) identifies as "spectator" or "participant" perspectives. For instance, two preservice teachers who self-described as middle-class or privileged described disadvantage in this manner:

Example 1:
Some of my students are profoundly disadvantaged. For example, one student told me of his mother who left him on the side of the road when he was 2 [years], and that he thinks this probably saved his life as she didn't look after him. That same student also believes that his current guardians do not like him. This student is disadvantaged *because he is entirely preoccupied with social-emotional issues* and *has an insecure attachment style* [emphasis added].

Example 2:
Some students who have no individual disadvantages are still, in my view, disadvantaged compared to their peers in higher SES [socioeconomic status] settings as their cultural capital is low and their peer group's level is several years behind the national average. Those students, who are the

high performing end of the class, are likely learning less than they are capable of *because they are in this community* and at this school *and with these students as classmates* [emphasis added].

Each of these statements seems, at first glance, informed, professional, and objective. The first looks at disadvantage through a predominantly psychological lens. Her analysis of her student appears to be evidence based. She draws on trauma-informed learning, viewing the student as "preoccupied" with complex emotional concerns and insecure in her attachments or abilities to relate to others. This diagnosis may be accurate but is not how someone would be likely to talk about themselves, and the impressions are deficit, identifying the student by what they lack or by their problem rather than through a strength-based lens. Demonstrating well-meaning discourses of communities who seem to be the problem itself, the teacher in Example 2 lays some blame at the feet of the students' own disadvantaged communities who, albeit without meaning to, bring themselves and other disadvantaged students down. The highly problematic belief in the "culture of poverty," a theory that originated in the 1960s, is still common; that is, disadvantaged students achieve less because of the values or behaviors of the communities they are from. The cultural deficit approach is "a model that situates students' 'disadvantage' in their culture (communities, families, ways of knowing, etc.) and thus views 'disadvantage' as a problem of socialization that can be overcome through compensatory programs" (Allweiss & Grant, 2013, p. 13).

The most normalized of the myths of cultures of poverty is that some groups of people, or some parents, do not care about or see the value in education. These perspectives are from the vantage points of people who represent dominant groups. A strengths-based perspective would look not at what people lack or do not have but would recognize the "funds of knowledge" or community knowledges held by all young people and their families, no matter their backgrounds. Rather than "places from which children must be saved or rescued," so-called disadvantaged communities "contain valuable knowledge and experiences that can foster educational development" (Moll & Gonzalez, 1997, p. 98). It seems self-evident to say there are always going to be blind spots in how people without lived experience interpret the lives of others. Teachers influence young peoples' lives and trajectories and have a responsibility to step back and listen.

In Contrast: Lived Experience

The caring but distanced perspectives of preservice teachers who have not personally experienced disadvantage are now contrasted with counternarratives from those with lived experiences of historical disadvantage. These preservice teachers and teachers often express much more discomfort with the stigma attached to the label disadvantage. Rather than feeling less-than, many of those we spoke to talked about disadvantage very differently, such as one person who came from a remote and socially isolated low socioeconomic regional Australian town who said,

> While [my background had] disadvantages, it also holds many advantages. We hold such a significant sense of community that borders on a sense of family. So I would not necessarily call us "disadvantaged" per se. Rather I would call us distinctive.

Another said,

> Disadvantaged is a concept that might provoke pitifulness, lack of access to education and other social services. It can be related to low income and high criminal rate communities. To me it can also represent a strength, which is translated into a burning personal drive.

These are clear examples of how disadvantage shifts to a strengths-based perspective when lived experience is taken into account (Vernikoff et al., 2022). Without denying structural and systemic exist, funds of knowledge such as community cohesion, strength of mind, and resourcefulness are emphasized. Firsthand interviews often focus on disadvantage in terms of social exclusion or as highlighting unequal access to power rather than as a personal trait or failing. Almost all our interviews with people who self-identified as disadvantaged made it clear that they had had to overcome barriers, but many, as one wrote, said things such as "I like the term 'obstacle' better because when we describe someone as disadvantaged, I think it puts a label on them and seems quite definite." This was often posed as a dilemma because none of these respondents wanted to pretend they had not experienced "hardship," yet most were very concerned about the label and what that might mean for how they were treated, their opportunities, and their futures and those of their children.

A dislike, a strong ambiguity of the "label," and rejection of the word was common, even among those who knew without a doubt that they had lived with such disadvantages as poverty, racism, ableism, social isolation, or a combination of other historically disadvantaging factors. Very few who said they had grown up with disadvantage suggested it did not exist—nobody wanted to make it invisible. However, the primary criticism around the use of the term was the implicit judgment it generated and the stigma associated with the word:

> Long story short, disadvantage to me comes in many forms. I consider myself privileged and lucky in some areas, but not in others. If the term isn't used to make a moral judgment or place limitations on someone, I have no issues with the term.

Similarly, another person interviewed said,

> This is a problematic word for me. Besides a real sense of lacking in some way it also forms an image of needing to be fixed by someone or something. I get that I may not have had "advantage" but I did have something that was worthy.

> It's like when people say about rural "it's in the middle of nowhere"—but it's somewhere for someone and so that needs to be acknowledged and respected. The trickier part is your question around what you would replace it with? If context matters, which I believe it does, then maybe something around that. I don't want to be called anything—I want to be able to feel as if I am supported to be all the me's I can be—and be given the options and visions.

The very real sense of ambiguity people felt about the term was summed up by others with lived experience, one of whom said, "I recognize that the term 'disadvantaged' can be stigmatizing, so the use of an alternative term is preferable." Another said, "I feel like I faced a double disadvantage—my condition, and then also the stigma of that condition."

As we have noted in earlier chapters, disadvantage is a hard word to replace. In a sense, it is useful as a way for schools and agencies to leverage funding to support good programs and financial support for families who need it. Naming and defining disadvantage is significant to redistribute resources. For instance, in the United States, the National School Lunch Program is dependent on measuring eligibility, and in the UK, the free school meal entitlement is a proxy for poverty. In Australia and elsewhere, schools that can identify themselves and their communities as disadvantaged are eligible to receive funding designed to make schools more equitable (Rowe & Perry, 2019). Declaring disadvantage is sometimes embarrassing or demeaning but cannot be avoided. This is understood by people with lived experience of disadvantage.

However, the acceptance of the term as necessary but sometimes damaging is often noticed with skepticism and resignation. As one person said,

> I couldn't shake the idea that it's a double-edged sword. You have to use that word because it has currency. You have to take on words like disadvantaged or low-socioeconomic because they're a gateway into support services like Centrelink or

food donations. But on the other hand it seems to focus a lot on the individuals who experience disadvantage than the system which creates it. I don't like the term as it's often equated to life experiences and conditions that the people in my family might feel privileged to have. Our situation is probably more like "complex poverty" mixed in with a lot of preventable but systemic violence and harm that a word like "disadvantaged" would prefer to ignore.

Additionally, frustration was expressed at the simplistic use of disadvantage. Many people pointed out that not all disadvantage is the same, and that it is layered, complex, and, while the word itself was not used, intersectional in nature. People generally qualified which kind of disadvantage they felt they had experienced, such as this preservice teacher who said,

> My family were very low middle class that had been dragged up by my dad's teaching work. This meant that I ended up in situations where I was at schools where I was one of the most disadvantaged in the room. We were not below the poverty line but I was certainly at a financial disadvantage compared to my peers. However, I had a roof over my head and healthy food. I did know this as a child because I'm trans. I deliberately did not come out until I was completely financially independent as I knew it would not be physically safe.

Furthermore, some people with lived experience specifically expressed concerns that the focus was on disadvantage rather than privilege:

> I think it's a polite white person thing to label a person or group disadvantaged. It's easier than saying I was born into privilege and have no idea what it means to face systemic discrimination based on your family's income, skin color, sexuality etc.

Statements such as these are reminders that teachers, such as those from privileged backgrounds, must be prepared to understand their own positionality—including their privilege—before embarking on assumptions about their students and their lives.

Nevertheless, despite considerable discomfort with being called disadvantaged, there was overwhelming agreement that schools and teachers should improve how teachers are prepared to work with young people and their families who are historically vulnerable and receive unequal school experiences and postschool opportunities, and for teachers to be better informed and safer in their practices. Teachers who listened to, advocated for, and practiced in ways that could affect change were remembered:

> I grew up financially advantaged, but emotionally disadvantaged due to issues associated with family conflict and sexual identity. In my teenage years, I did not recognise my circumstances as being disadvantageous—I just felt angry, depressed and confused. School was somewhat of a safe place for me away from the troubles at home. A greater recognition of my circumstances may have made my journey less difficult.

In this primary research, we were able to focus directly on the keyword disadvantage in an effort to consider its use as a term and its drawbacks, hindrances, and benefits to those who "wear" the label. Effecting change requires a more engaged dialogue with "disadvantaged" populations who are experts in their own experiences.

Conclusion

One of the difficulties of including firsthand accounts in teacher education is the risk of engaging in what Garthwaite (2016) refers to as "poverty porn." A UK series *Benefits Street* filmed families in poverty to show what their lives were "really like." Similarly, in Australia, a documentary TV series *Struggle Street* followed several families living with disadvantage in ways Lawton (2020) called sensationalized, voyeuristic, and stereotyped. We believe teacher educators should introduce preservice teachers to the lived experiences of young people and families who daily experience the effects of disadvantage but with a caveat. Teacher educators themselves (or ourselves) may have not experienced disadvantage firsthand, and if they (we) do introduce lived experiences to their preservice teachers, we must do so with ethics, care, and caution.

CHAPTER FIVE

Praxis, Hope, and Innovative Strategies for Preservice Teachers

Introduction

We end this book with a discussion of how the keyword *disadvantage* informs how teachers are currently prepared. This final chapter merges theory and practice, offering illustrative case studies of three initial teacher education programs that have been designed to prepare teachers to understand the complexities of disadvantage, including the use of the word itself. These case studies describe programs from different countries—Australia, Finland, and Spain—that contribute to broadening our understanding of how to prepare teachers to critically rethink and deal with disadvantage across three different locations.

So, our aim in this chapter is to tackle the challenge of educating democratic and courageous teachers who understand—and can push back against—inequities that impact their students, families, and the communities in which they will teach. For that purpose, it is essential that teacher students reflect critically, within a historical and cultural context, on the use of the word disadvantage. This means that teacher education should not render disadvantage invisible but instead help students see it, name it, and fight it. Some societies are seemingly so equal that disadvantage gets hidden and silenced. We argue that the fight is *especially* important in those societies.

The selected case studies of initial teacher education and school-based programs, those from Australia, Finland, and Spain, have been designed to name and address disadvantage in their own contexts. In doing so, these cases do not introduce discourses that may reproduce disadvantage itself. Instead, they create affordances for preservice teachers to name the word in dialogue with others; hence, they name the world to change it (Freire, 2000). We consider these cases as locally shaped examples of praxis where future teachers engage in reflection and action, not only to name the disadvantage, but also to act against the inequities that are still excluding many children and youth worldwide.

This chapter is informed by notions of praxis and hope, especially drawing on the work of Paulo Freire. Indeed, in his *Pedagogy of the Oppressed* (2000), Freire argued that "human activity is theory and practice; it is reflection and action. It cannot ... be reduced to either verbalism or activism" (p. 125). Only in a process of "true praxis," Freire argues, can people leave behind the status of the "objects" to assume the status of the historical "subjects" (p. 160). This approach is essential for educators to introduce them to a critical form of thinking about their pedagogical practice and about the world, in which they need hope. As Freire states, "One of the tasks of the progressive educator is to unveil opportunities for hope, no matter what the obstacles may be" (p. 9). Through a Freirean lens, we must understand education and the struggle for improving it from a place of hopes and dreams, since hope is understood as an ontological need.

Both concepts, hope and praxis, are essential for change and equity. In the struggle for social change, hope is essential, but it is not enough; it also needs praxis to accomplish concrete changes. In Freire's view, praxis is about action and about change. For him, there is "no dichotomy by which this praxis could be divided into a prior stage of reflection and a subsequent stage of action. Action and reflection occur simultaneously" (p. 128).

The origins of the word *praxis* go further back in history than Freire. For Aristotle, the Greek word praxis (πρᾶξις) meant doing something good or virtuous, with good aims. Praxis was thus led by practical wisdom, i.e., *phronesis*, that helped the doer to consider these aims. This kind of wisdom differs from wisdom based purely on concrete or technical actions, or *techné*. In the nineteenth century, Karl Marx interpreted the ideal praxis in his vision for an equal, better world order. The neo-Marxist idea of praxis is about free and creative practice through which humans differentiate themselves from other animals and make a difference in the world; it is "history-making action" (Kemmis, 2014, p. 26), which may have implications for good or ill. In all praxis definitions, the emphasis is on the active mode of human practice. Drawing mostly on Aristotle and Marx, Mahon et al. (2019) summarize different views on praxis, saying that it is "about acting in the world in a way that contributes positively and meaningfully to society, or acting in the interests of humankind" (p. 464).

Few writings on praxis, and certainly not the older ones by Aristotle, have done much to address disadvantage in relation to people's backgrounds, such as ethnicity and gender. Freire wrote about inequities due to people's economic situation, as did Marx in his discussion about the rights of workers. All these (male) theorists have been criticized for overlooking people's differences, especially those of gender or ethnicity (Ellsworth, 1989; Weiler, 1991). On the other hand, Freire's work has also been seen as foundational for later feminist movements. His points about the oppressed/oppressor, a binary situation in which we are all enmeshed, as well as the crucial need to break the culture of silence about inequity, have been extended by feminist scholars (Stromquist, 2014). Likewise, Marx points out that people's relationships with one another are a result of their roles in economic life and that relations of production divide humans into competing classes, e.g., workers and bosses. As Brown (2014) notes, "Even though Marx did not write a great deal on gender, and did not develop a systematic theory of gender and the family, it was, for him, an essential category for understanding the division of labor, production, and society in general" (p. 56). Chapter 2 discussed this point further and highlighted why an intersectional lens on disadvantage is so crucial and how the core idea of praxis can be seen as being in line with, and in fact an inspiration for, the ideas of intersectionality.

Naming disadvantage in the preparation of future teachers implies the need to engage in critical reflection and action— to take a stand against injustice. This prevents us from participating in discourses of disadvantage that stigmatize others or that become tokenistic language. Instead, praxis becomes an ongoing process of reflection and action that transforms our understanding of disadvantage and empowers teachers to orient themselves toward educational and social transformation with a sense of hope to counteract inequities. The three examples we provide illustrate this.

Strategies for Preservice Teachers

The case studies in this chapter come from Australia, Finland, and Spain. Their societies are different, as are their educational systems, as we briefly show before each case. In all systems, however, the publicly announced aim of education is to level disadvantage and foster equity. Each of these countries has also created specific programs that train preservice teachers to name and address disadvantages. They all serve as excellent examples of how theory and practice can be linked across contextual differences—how it is possible to aim for the same outcome (leveling disadvantage) when the starting points are very different.

The closest Finnish equivalent for the English word disadvantage is *huono-osaisuus*. In translation, this refers to someone who has ended up in an unfavorable position in the world and its meaning in research mostly links to multifaceted economic, social, and health/well-being issues (Saari, 2015). The word has been criticized for being problem centered or deficit, and it definitely is—its sole purpose is to name a problem, disadvantage. However, the useful way to use the Finnish term *huono-osaisuus* is to point to the *extra-individual* or external problems related to equity rather than to blame individuals for their problems.

The word disadvantage translates as *desfavorecido* in Spanish, but it is not used as an equivalent to the English word. Similar to the Finnish case, the translation into Spanish is not equivalent to the English word, and its meaning mainly emphasizes socioeconomic deprivation. But when used in education, it also implies a deficit view that blames the families and the students who suffer the consequences of marginalization and exclusion.

We now turn to the case studies, giving a short background of each context and one or two examples of how disadvantage has been addressed in teacher education. We conclude by arguing that building on some of the central ideas in these programs can offer teacher education, and indeed our whole educational systems, hope.

Equity-Oriented Teachers in Australia

Australia has an explicit agenda to produce equity-oriented teachers who engage in inclusive practice that promotes equitable outcomes for students. This includes being able to teach diverse learners, including Aboriginal and Torres Strait Islander students, and contributing to closing the achievement gap. These goals are expressed through federal and state-based educational policy and by the most recent *Report of the Quality*

Initial Teacher Education Review (Department of Education, Skills and Employment, 2022) that emphasizes, among other things, the need for teachers who are culturally responsive, understand trauma-informed learning, and can teach in ways that ameliorate the effects of disadvantage. The *Alice Springs (Mparntwe) Education Declaration* (Department of Education, Skills and Employment, 2019) prioritizes support for all young Australians at risk of disadvantage, stating,

> Targeted support can help learners such as those from low socioeconomic backgrounds, those from regional, rural, and remote areas, migrants and refugees, learners in out of home care, homeless young people, and children with disability to reach their potential. This means tailoring to the needs of individuals across a system that prioritises equity of opportunity and that supports achievement.
>
> (p. 17)

In its vision for Australia, the declaration sets a challenge for teacher education and teachers, with the explicitly stated understanding that education can transform lives.

Globally, of course, educational disadvantage has been exacerbated through the COVID-19 pandemic. Whatever disadvantage students faced previously has been compounded, and furthermore, Australia is facing unprecedented teacher shortages as teachers "burn out," and fewer people in Australia apply to become teachers at all. With fewer teachers entering the profession, encouraging the most socially just, community-engaged teachers to work in the hardest-to-staff schools is even more important. There is an urgent need to address what Domina et al. (2017) call "teacher sorting," whereby the "best" teachers are courted by and end up employed in middle-class or private schools, where teachers in low socioeconomic schools are more transient and teach out of their subject areas much more often. All of this has a flow-on effect on student outcomes, teacher morale, and community reputation.

Nexus Initial Teacher Education Program

There have been many attempts in initial teacher education over the years to prepare high-content, social-justice-oriented teachers who not only have a lifelong commitment to working with so-called disadvantaged communities but who are also grounded in enough theory to critically reflect on their own practice and vice versa. Identifies the aspect of explicit pedagogy as moral work. The dilemma of how to bridge theory and practice is noted by many social justice education scholars. Margaret Robinson (2020) responds to the fact that many preservice teachers can identify theory and concepts related to disadvantage but indicate they "did not feel prepared in a practical sense" (p. 27) as an issue of ethical agency. One program that attempts to merge theory and practice through what Robinson calls "situational learning" (p. 16) is the National Exceptional Teaching for Disadvantaged Schools (NETDS) project (Burnett & Lampert, 2019), an undergraduate teacher education program that matches preservice teachers with schools in a highly mentored, equity-based program. Another is La Trobe University's federally and state-funded, employment-based Nexus pathway where, continuing the theme of praxis, preservice teachers are embedded in and employed by hard-to-staff partner schools in the state of Victoria. Unlike some other initial teacher education programs for high achievers, Nexus prioritizes preservice teachers who themselves come from cultural and linguistic diversity, including Indigenous backgrounds, or have grown up in urban or regional hard-to-staff, high-poverty, or disadvantaged communities. In Nexus, participants are paid as part-time education support staff workers (or "teachers' aides") while they study, engaging fortnightly in regular drop-ins where they reflect on such diverse topics as privilege, youth homelessness, Indigenous education, LGBTQI+ safe schools and more. A feature of this program is the "lived experience" sessions based on the human libraries that started in Denmark. In these online and face-to-face sessions, future teachers have the opportunity to talk to community members who have experienced such issues as food and housing insecurity or who come from historically marginalized community groups. As a community-engaged teacher education program, this provides a rare opportunity for teachers to go beyond the school walls in their teacher preparation and ask whatever they like. This community-engaged element of Nexus is one Australian example of a pedagogy of hope. Most crucially, the pedagogy of hope represented by initial teacher education programs such as the NETDS project or Nexus lies in how they mobilize preservice teachers who have shown a predisposition toward social justice (Lampert & Browne, 2022) and subsequently gives them deep opportunities to strengthen their knowledge and commitment. Nexus centralizes critical reflection, community engagement, and fostering deep awareness community funds of knowledge no matter where and in what contexts participants teach. These are strengths-based programs designed to prepare graduate teachers to understand and enact principles of social justice.

Equity and Disadvantage in Finland

The Finnish example has quite different starting points. Regardless of what is measured, Finland tends to be among the top three countries in rankings of student performance, such as the Organisation for Economic Co-operation and Development's (OECD's), Programme for International Student Assessment (PISA), as well as rankings measuring equity (Ahonen, 2021). Finland rates highly when the focus is on the equity between genders, between poor and rich, and on other social, ethnic, religious, and cultural measures. Finland has also repeatedly been ranked as the happiest country in the *World Happiness Report* (Helliwell et al., 2021). However, measured success, happiness, or equity does not mean that disadvantage does not exist in Finnish society or Finnish schools. Finland's success in equity measurements means that disadvantage might be harder to notice.

Leveling disadvantage has been the aim of Finnish schools from very early on. In the nineteenth century, Finland's educational system had two streams, *kansakoulu* ("people's school") and *oppikoulu* ("learning school"). The people's school was open for all, and it became mandatory in 1921, shortly after Finland's independence. The development of a national school system was motivated by Finland's need to separate from the Swedish and Russian systems. The task was challenging as Finland was an extremely poor country with major regional differences. The Russian government, which ruled Finland until its independence in 1917, did not put a lot of effort into developing Finland as it was remote and mostly rural. The national school system was needed to gather all children together, foster regional development, and raise the "national spirit" of Finland at the emergence of its independence. One of the innovative and revolutionary aspects of this new system was its free hot lunch for all, which worked to get the poor children to school. Finland was the first country in the world to make free school lunch mandatory, just after the Second War World in 1948, and the school lunch program is still in place.

The Finnish school system was a good start, but it did not solve the problem of inequity between different groups within Finland. The dual system of the people's school and the learning school was phased out in the 1970s in favor of a more equal and comprehensive system. This marked the start of the development of the current comprehensive school of Finland, where Grades 1 to 9 are mandatory and the curriculum broad and flexible, but it is the same for all. This reform was guided by the aim of equity, and the way to reach it was to balance differences in resources related to children's unequal backgrounds, equalizing opportunities and providing all children the same chances to educate themselves further. This has mostly worked well. Sahlberg (201) argues that the Finnish education sector development has been grounded on equal opportunities for all, equitable distribution of resources rather than competition, intensive early interventions for prevention, and building gradual trust among education practitioners, especially teachers. But does this mean Finland is without disadvantage? More critical voices rightly point out that it means disadvantage is hidden, but it is not nonexistent (Huilla, 2022).

Disadvantage in Finland most often refers to where people live. Segregation between suburbs and schools is modest compared to many other countries, but the situation is changing: The number of families living below the relative poverty line is now three times higher than in the 1990s (Salmi, 2020), and the situation has remained consistent (Kallio & Hakovirta, 2020; Saari, 2015). As we write this in 2022, the war in Ukraine has caused an unprecedented increase in the price of food and energy all over Europe, making the situation for the poor even harder. Finnish schools in disadvantaged areas can get equity funding or more resources for supporting students, but some argue that the solutions are too local and temporary, overlooking the issues that reach beyond schools to societies (Huilla, 2022). The other significant cause of disadvantage in Finnish schools is that the education system is only starting to learn how to address diversity. The Finnish school system has been planned with a mainstream, middle-class Finnish family in mind. The percentage of children born outside Finland has increased from 2 percent at the time when the Finnish comprehensive school was started in the 1970s to approximately 7 percent today (Finnish Immigration Service, 2022). But of course, Finnish schools have always been diverse, and disadvantage in Finnish schools is not only about ethnic background, but also about wealth, gender, and a number of other intersecting factors.

Intercultural Teacher Education Program, Finland

The Intercultural Teacher Education program (originally Multicultural Education program) at Oulu University was founded at the beginning of the 1990s by Rauni Räsänen as an action research project. The need for intercultural teacher education was based on the notion that the world is changing, one size does not fit all, and there is diversity even in the seemingly homogenous groups of Finnish schools. Importantly, the program was truly planned as praxis, putting theories in practice. One of its core aims was to add elements of human rights, ethics, and globalization into the Finnish teacher education curriculum so that future teachers could develop skills that were useful in the changing world. Those elements are still integrated into all the courses in the program.

The Intercultural Teacher Education program has become one of Finland's longest running and most popular teacher education programs with a special focus. The program's aims remain as timely as ever: to name and address disadvantages that might be hard for preservice teachers to see and to continuously change to address new challenges. Importantly, the program does not just focus on a single challenge of equity—for example, that of poverty or increasing migration in Finland; students on the program engage with real-world problems and invent solutions to them. The program has long-lasting collaborations with organizations working with refugees and asylum seekers, gender and sexual minorities, and victims of domestic violence, and new connections are created with each new group of students. Such work serves to prepare critical, active teachers for the changing world, but it is rarely included in the packed curricula of regular teacher education programs in Finland. Bringing theory and practice together and reflecting on the latest developments in society has meant, for example, recent foci on online teaching due to the COVID-19 pandemic and developing educational materials for a new group in a potentially disadvantaged position in Finland: the thousands of Ukrainian children who have arrived in Finland in 2022.

The Intercultural Teacher Education program is a fruitful example to consider teacher education in this chapter as it has been developed in one of the most equal countries in the world, but it still hopes to address disadvantages that remain hidden until they are named and addressed. The fact that it has existed for three decades despite frequent changes in teacher education shows that it has been needed.

Tackling Inequities in Spain

Preparing teachers to successfully tackle and address inequities in Spain is a challenge, which has not been addressed in initial teacher training programs. Despite efforts to improve teacher education in the last decades, there are no specific strategies in the programs to equip teachers with the skills and knowledge to work in schools and communities located in contexts of poverty and social disadvantage. A ten-year analysis of initial teacher training programs for primary and secondary teachers in Spain found no reference to disadvantage or to students with minority backgrounds (Manso, 2019). This is also absent from Spanish educational policies that establish the competencies teachers must acquire during initial teacher education. This becomes even more problematic when preparing secondary teachers who, after a one-year training program, may end up working in disadvantaged schools without knowing anything about the communities they are in.

One of the most disadvantaged populations in Spain that our future teachers will encounter and work with are the Roma people. The Roma people are the largest ethnic minority in Europe, with up to 12 million living across the continent and about 80 percent of them living below the poverty line (European Union Agency for Fundamental Rights [FRA], 2016). Despite efforts to ensure equal access to education, the Roma in Spain and elsewhere suffer from segregation in schools, poor-quality housing, and high unemployment rates, among other problems (Flecha et al., 2022). In particular, Roma students are disproportionately allocated in special schools and classes for children with "mild mental disabilities." When placed in regular classrooms, Roma children arguably have access to a limited curriculum and receive overall low-quality schooling (Díez-Palomar et al., 2018). This is caused by the fact that teachers tend to have low expectations of Roma children, and discriminatory attitudes are common in schools and societies (Alexiadou, 2019). Indeed, for most preservice teachers, Roma students are invisible during their training. This absence perpetuates prejudices about Roma students and their families, with students and families blamed for a lack of interest in education. Alternatively, this apparent lack of interest is considered to be part of their culture (Vargas & Gómez, 2003). To tackle this situation, CREA (Community of Research on Excellence for All) researchers have developed and implemented Dialogic Gatherings in initial teacher education across several universities in Spain. These gatherings engage students in critical reflection about how to name and address disadvantage in different contexts and with different populations, considering its multidimensionality and intersectionality.

Dialogic Gatherings in Teacher Education

Dialogic Gatherings (Flecha and Soler, 2013) are a successful educational action where participants read and reflect on many of the most significant cultural works of humankind, which leads to a dialogic construction of knowledge among participants. In Dialogic Gatherings, participants share knowledge and make meaning of the same text on the basis of the principle of egalitarian dialogue, which underpins the conversation. Before the gathering, student teachers agreed on the text the entire group will read before the gathering.

Everyone reads the text and selects any ideas, sentences, or paragraphs that appeal to them. Then, during the gathering, they share those ideas and their reasons for choosing them with the rest of the group. The idea is that everyone contributes and shares their views and arguments. This egalitarian space fosters openness to listening to others and to reducing the hierarchical approaches to teaching and learning (Barros del Río et al., 2021).

When working with preservice teachers to address the issue of disadvantage, Dialogic Gatherings include reading and discussing academic articles or other texts focusing on improving the education and lives of those named as disadvantaged. Providing future teachers with research that demonstrates its benefits and relevance for educational practice seems essential to achieve social impact (García-Carrión et al., 2020). At the University of Deusto, Dialogic Gatherings were implemented weekly with students of the Master of Secondary Education, a one-year program required to become secondary teachers.

One of the most impactful readings was "Turning Difficulties Into Possibilities: Engaging Roma Families and Students in School Through Dialogic Learning" by Flecha and Soler (2013). The article was awarded the *Cambridge Journal of Education*'s Best Paper Prize 2013 and was helpful for understanding the inequalities that impact Roma students. The Dialogic Gathering of this article allowed student teachers to reflect on their (lack of) knowledge of the Roma people, as well as to encourage them to challenge some of the prejudices they perhaps did not even know they had. The discussion was not just an empty discourse; instead, some of the students made sense of the reading by connecting it with their own experiences in the community-based schools where they were doing their internships. This allowed for an experience of praxis, including reflection and action.

Another important piece used in the program was Freire's (2005) work *Teachers as Cultural Workers: Letters to Those Who Dare Teach* (Freire, 2005), which challenges students to reflect critically on disadvantage and the act of teaching. In these Dialogic Gatherings, interactions among preservice teachers create opportunities for students to critically reflect not only on the history of exclusion and discrimination against disadvantaged communities, but also on how to counteract oppression through education. On the one hand, preservice teachers reflect on critical theories and research evidence to challenge oppression, and on the other, they connect such knowledge with their own lives and experiences, making meaning and creating a space for action and hope. Among the dialogues that emerged in the Dialogic Gatherings, participants focused on teacher skills and values, their roles as teachers, and their social selves to intervene as agents of change. This dialogic context creates affordances for participation and critical thinking (Simpson, 2016) and for educated hope. Through Dialogic Gatherings, student teachers can act as "active epistemic agents" (Skidmore, 2006, p. 505), having the opportunities to share their own knowledge, values, and beliefs through reflection and action.

Teacher Education, Praxis, and Hope

The Nexus-program in Australia, the Intercultural Teacher Education program of Oulu, Finland, and the Dialogic Gatherings in Spain all have the same aim—to level disadvantage in their respective educational contexts. They all have their own ways of doing that, each having developed them to suit the purposes in those countries.

At its core, the Australian Nexus program aims to prepare teachers with a deep understanding of the causes of poverty, disadvantage, and inequity. While preservice teachers complete a university-situated mainstream Master of Teaching, they engage weekly in additional community-led discussion groups and professional development of topics such as trauma-informed learning, anti-racism education, LGBTQI+ safe schools and consent learning, and many other opportunities. By spending as much time employed in "disadvantaged" schools as in university classes, participants engage in constant praxis, applying what they learn in theory in "real-life" practice. In addition, Nexus participants are given preference when they themselves come from culturally diverse, Indigenous, and disadvantaged backgrounds (urban, rural, or remote) to attract teachers to the profession who deeply understand the communities in which they will teach.

In Finland, one of the original aims of the Intercultural Teacher Education program was to make disadvantage visible in a context well known for its equity. During the course of almost three decades of its existence, the program has educated critical and active teachers, educational leaders, and researchers, ready to identify new issues to be tackled. Some of the student initiatives that started as student projects have turned into educational products or established practices. These include, for example, educational materials for Roma languages and culture and an app to help asylum seekers find work, education, or volunteering opportunities in Finland. In addition to serving as teachers in Finland, graduates from the Intercultural Teacher Education program have found their way to schools in different parts of the world, refugee camps, politics, and research, to name just a few fields of work. Importantly, the program does not bring additional costs or burdens to the university. Students cover all areas of the general teacher education program, the only difference being that the core elements have been reshaped with equity and ethics in mind.

In Spain, Dialogic Gatherings have created a unique dialogic space in mainstream initial teacher education, where the issue of disadvantaged has been absent from the official curriculum in higher education. This strategy has contributed not only to tackling the issue of historically marginalized communities, such as the Roma, migrants, or children living in poverty, in the discourse, but also to providing teachers with the scientific knowledge to act against inequity. By reading and discussing educational research and theories with social impact and oriented to social change, student teachers are equipped with a "language of possibility" (Freire & Macedo, 1987) that encourages them to transform schools and communities into more inclusive, cohesive, and equal places. The collective meaning the group creates from the text is built upon their life experiences and is oriented to transform the educational and social inequalities the most vulnerable face.

These examples combine the notions of praxis and hope. They equip future teachers with critical knowledge to see and name disadvantage and provide teachers with the skills and courage to act against it. Importantly, they encourage future teachers to engage with the communities they are going to work with. A combination of exposure and mentored opportunities for critical reflection reduces biases, and personal experiences with different groups help preservice teachers to understand the mechanisms of disadvantage from their points of view. This contact also allows preservice teachers to develop a "sense of hope" (Freire, 1992) and what Maureen Robinson (2020, p. 28) calls a "sense of ethical agency" to intervene and change those structures through praxis.

Conclusion

In this book we have examined the complex meanings and implications of the concept of disadvantage and how these play out in teacher education and in the schooling of students who are fixed with this label. We have argued that the concept of disadvantage and how it is employed in education is highly problematic for it potentially stigmatizes the very groups of students that it is designed to support. Yet we also note that simplistic solutions, such as not using the term "disadvantage" are not helpful for this conceals the very issues that need to be confronted. Instead, we contend that teacher education needs to prepare preservice teachers with critical understandings of disadvantage. In this book we have provided examples of programs that aim to do precisely that. As societies become more diverse and inequitable, the challenges in schools grow. We conclude by noting that schools and teachers cannot be the complete solution to the complex issues that challenge our societies. However, as Fischman (2009, p. 209) reminds us, "we must be explicit in our articulation of pedagogies of freedom and hope."

In the first chapter of this book, we posed some questions. Now, at the end of this book, we revisit and add to these questions:

1　What is the aim of using the word disadvantage, and who defines it? Why does this matter?

2　Would changing the language of disadvantage be transformative or regressive? Would it lead to better practice? How can theory and practice around disadvantage be merged for teachers to transform education?

3　Whose purpose does the language of disadvantage serve, when, and why? What language is used in your context and what effects does that language produce?

4　If the word is replaced with something more transformative, what would that be? What would be lost and what would be gained? How would you know?

We encourage you as a reader to consider: Have your responses changed? Can you pose additional questions? Can you use the ideas presented in this book to develop a reflexive practice that could level disadvantage in your context? We hope this book gives tools for educators around the world to continue exploring the keyword disadvantage in their professional lives into the future.

NOTES

Chapter 4

1   Australian Ethics approval HEC18117, La Trobe University, Australia.

REFERENCES

Ahonen, A. K. (2021). Finland: Success through equity: The trajectories in PISA performance. In N. Crato (Ed.), *Improving a country's education* (pp. 121–36). Springer, Cham. https://doi.org/10.1007/978-3-030-59031-4_6

Albanese, A. (2022, May 22). Incoming prime minister Anthony Albanese's full speech after Labor wins federal election. *ABC News*. https://www.abc.net.au/news/2022-05-22/anthony-albanese-acceptance-speech-full-transcript/101088736

Alexiadou, N. (2019). Framing education policies and transitions of Roma students in Europe. *Comparative Education*, 55(3), 422–42.

Allweiss, A., & Grant, C. A. (2013). Progressives, conservatives and "educational disadvantage": The limits of the bifurcation. *Race, Gender & Class*, 20(1/2), 8–24. http://www.jstor.org/stable/43496902

Apple, M. W. (2013). *Can education change society?* Routledge.

Arabena, K. (2017, August 28). Discourses and impact: How linguistic responsibility can help "close the gap". *Croakey*. https://www.croakey.org/discourses-and-impact-how-linguistic-responsibility-can-help-close-the-gap/

Australian Government (2020). *Closing the Gap*. Department of the Prime Minister and Cabinet. https://www.niaa.gov.au/sites/default/files/publications/closing-the-gap-report-2020.pdf

Australian Institute for Teaching and School Leadership (AITSL) (2018). *Professional standards for teachers*.

Bakali, N. (2016). Unveiling the lived realities of Muslim female students in Canadian secondary schools. In Bakali, N. (Ed.), *Islamophobia. Transgressions: Cultural studies and education* (pp. 83–99). Sense Publishers. https://doi.org/10.1007/978-94-6300-779-5_6

Barros-del rio, M. A., Álvarez, P., & Molina Roldán, S. (2021). Implementing dialogic gatherings in TESOL teacher education. *Innovation in Language Learning and Teaching*, 15(2), 169–80.

Bernelius, V., & Kosunen, S. (2023). "Three bedrooms and a nice school"—Residential choices, school choices and vicious circles of segregation in the education landscape of Finnish cities. In Thrupp, M., Seppänen, P., Kauko, J., & Kosunen, S. (Eds.), *Finland's famous education system* (pp. 175–91). Singapore: Springer.

Bibby, T., Lupton, R., & Raffo, C. (2017). *Responding to poverty and disadvantage in schools a reader for teachers*. London: Palgrave Macmillan.

Blair, K., Dunn, K., Kamp, A., & Alam, O. (2017). *Challenging racism project 2015–16* (National survey report). Western Sydney University. https://www.westernsydney.edu.au/__data/assets/pdf_file/0009/1201203/OMAC1694_Challenging_Racism_Report_4_-_FINAL.pdf

Boddy, J. (2019). Troubling meanings of "family" for young people who have been in care: From policy to lived experience. *Journal of Family Issues*, 40(16), 2239–63. https://doi.org/10.1177/0192513X18808564

Boler, M. (1999). *Feeling power: Emotions and education*. Taylor & Francis.

Bomer, R., Dworin, J., May, L., & Semingson, P. (2008). Miseducating teachers about the poor: A critical analysis of Ruby Payne. *Teachers College Record*, 110(12), 2497–531.

Bottomley, G. (1976). Ethnicity and identity among Greek Australians. *Australian and New Zealand Journal of Sociology*, 12(2), 118–25. https://doi.org/10.1177/144078337601200208

Brewer, T. J. (2014). Accelerated burnout: How Teach for America's academic impact model and theoretical culture of accountability can foster disillusionment among its corps members. *Educational Studies*, 50, 246–63.

Brown, H. (2014). Marx on gender and the family. A summary. *Monthly Review: An Independent Socialist Magazine* 66, 48–57.

Brownlees, L., & Finch, N. (2010). Levelling the playing field. A UNICEF UK report into provision of services to unaccompanied or separated migrant children in three local authority areas in England. *UNICEF*. http://www.unicef.org.uk/Documents/Publications/levelling-playing-field.pdf

Burnett, B., & Lampert, J. (2019). The Australian national exceptional teaching for disadvantaged schools programme: A reflection on its first 8 years. *Journal of Education for Teaching*, 45(1), 31–46.

Carter, P., & Darling-Hammond, L. (2016). Teaching diverse learners. *Handbook of research on teaching*, 5, 593–638.

Change.org. (n.d.). *Western Sydney University condemns Pru Goward*. https://www.change.org/p/wsu-community-western-sydney-university-condemn-pru-goward

Cheng, A., & Peterson, P. (2021). Experimentally estimated impacts of school vouchers on educational attainments of moderately and severely disadvantaged students. *Sociology of Education*, 94(2), 159–74.

Chiang, H. S., Clark, M. A., & McConnell, S. (2017). Supplying disadvantaged schools with effective teachers: Experimental evidence on secondary math teachers from Teach for America. *Journal of Policy Analysis and Management*, 36(1), 97–125.

Chilisa, B., & Tsheko, G. N. (2014). Mixed methods in indigenous research: Building relationships for sustainable intervention outcomes. *Journal of Mixed Methods Research*, 8(3), 222–33.

Clarke, M., & Moore, A. (2013). Professional standards, teacher identities and an ethics of singularity. *Cambridge Journal of Education*, 43(4), 487–500.

Cochran-Smith, M., Villegas, A. M., Abrams, L., Chavez Moreno, L., Mills, T., & Stern, R. (2016). Research on teacher preparation: Charting the landscape of a sprawling field. *Handbook of Research on Teaching*, 5, 439–547.

Collins, P. H. (2000). *Black feminist thought: Knowledge, consciousness, and the politics of empowerment* (rev. ed.). Routledge.

Collins, P. H., & Chepp, V. (2013). Intersectionality. In G. Waylen, K. Celis, J. Kantola, & S. L. Weldon (Eds.), *The Oxford handbook of gender and politics* (57–87). https://doi.org/10.1093/oxfordhb/9780199751457.013.0002

Committee for Economic Development in Australia (CEDA) (2015). *Addressing entrenched disadvantage in Australia*. Committee for Economic Development.

Connell, R. W., White, V. M., & Johnston, K. M. (1992). An experiment in justice: The Disadvantaged Schools Program and the question of poverty, 1974–1990. *British Journal of Sociology of Education*, 13(4), 447–64. https://doi.org/10.1080/0142569920130404

Conus, X., & Fahrni, L. (2019). Routine communication between teachers and parents from minority groups: An endless misunderstanding? *Educational Review*, 71(2), 234–56. https://doi.org/10.1080/00131911.2017.1387098

Correa-Velez, I., Gifford, S. M., McMichael, C., & Sampson, R. (2017). Predictors of secondary school completion among refugee youth 8–9 years after resettlement in Melbourne, Australia. *Journal of International Migration and Integration*, 18(3), 791–805.

Corrigan, P. (2017). Beware the pity narrative. *Stigma and Health*, 2(2), 81–2. https://doi.org/10.1037/sah0000050

Crawford-Garrett, K., Oldham, S., & Thomas, M. A. M. (2021). Maintaining meritocratic mythologies: Teach for America and Ako Mātātupu: Teach First New Zealand. *Comparative Education*, 57(3), 360–76.

Crenshaw, K. (1989). Demarginalizing the intersection of race and sex: A Black feminist critique of antidiscrimination doctrine, feminist theory and antiracist politics. *University of Chicago Legal Forum*, 139–67.

Crenshaw, K. (1991). Mapping the margins: Intersectionality, identity politics, and violence against Women of Color. *Stanford Law Review*, 43(6), 1241–99. https://doi.org/10.2307/1229039

Davidson, P., Saunders, P., Bradbury, B., & Wong, M. (2020). *Poverty in Australia* 2020: *Part 1, overview*. (ACOSS/UNSW Poverty and Inequality Partnership Report No. 3). ACOSS.

Department of Education, Skills and Employment (2019). *The Alice Springs (Mparntwe) Education Declaration*. DESE, Australian Government.

Department of Education, Skills and Employment (2022). *Next steps: Report of the quality initial teacher education review*. DESE, Australian Government.

Díez-Palomar, J., Flecha, A., García-Carrión, R., & Molina-Roldán, S. (2018). Pathways to equitable and sustainable education through the inclusion of Roma students in learning mathematics. *Sustainability*, 10(7), 2191.

Domina, T., Penner, A., & Penner, E. (2017). Categorical inequality: Schools as sorting machines. *Annual Review of Sociology*, 43(1), 311–30.

Dumenden, I. (2014). *The soft bigotry of low expectations: The refugee student and mainstream schooling* [Doctoral dissertation]. La Trobe University.

Dunwoodie, K., Kaukko, M., Wilkinson, J., Reimer, K., & Webb, S. (2020). Widening university access for students of asylum-seeking backgrounds: (Mis)recognition in an Australian context. *Higher Education Policy*, 33(2), 243–64. https://doi.org/10.1057/s41307-019-00176-8

El Ashmawi, Y. (2016). *Testimonios of American Muslim parents* [Doctoral dissertation]. New Mexico State University.

Ellis, S., Thompson, I., McNicholl, J. & Thomson, J. (2016). Student teachers' perceptions of the effects of poverty on learner's educational attainment and well-being: Perspectives from England and Scotland. *Journal for Education and Teaching*, 42(4), 483–99. https://doi.org/10.1080/02607476.2016.1215542

Ellsworth, E. (1989). Why doesn't this feel empowering? Working through the repressive myths of critical pedagogy. *Harvard Educational Review*, 59(3), 297–324.

Elton-Chalcraft, S., Lander, V., Revell, L., Warner, D., & Whitworth, L. (2017). To promote, or not to promote fundamental British values? Teachers' standards, diversity and teacher education. *British Educational Research Journal*, 43(1), 29–48.

European Commission (2019). *A meta-evaluation of interventions for Roma inclusion.*

European Union Agency for Fundamental Rights (FRA) (2016, November 29). *80% of Roma are at risk of poverty, new survey finds.* [Press release]. http://fra.europa.eu/en/press-release/2016/80-roma-are-risk-poverty-new-survey-finds

Fincher, R., & Saunders, P. (2020). *Creating unequal futures: Rethinking poverty, inequality and disadvantage.* Routledge.

Fischman, G. (2009). Afterward. In Macrine, S. (Ed.), *Critical pedagogy in uncertain times.* New York: Palgrave Macmillan.

Flecha, & Soler, M. (2013). Turning difficulties into possibilities: engaging Roma families and students in school through dialogic learning. *Cambridge Journal of Education*, 43(4), 451–65.

Flecha, A., Abad-Merino, S., Macías-Aranda, F., & Segovia-Aguilar, B. (2022). Roma university students in Spain: Who are they? *Education Sciences*, 12(6), 400.

Flores-Crespo, P. (2007). Ethnicity, identity and educational achievement in Mexico. *International Journal of Educational Development*, 27(3), 331–9.

Fraser, N. (1997). *Justice interruptus.* Routledge.

Freire, P. (1973). *Education for critical consciousness.* Seabury Press.

Freire, P. (1992). *Pedagogy of hope*. Continuum.

Freire, P. (1997). *Pedagogy of the heart*. Continuum.

Freire, P. (2000). *Pedagogy of the oppressed* (30th anniversary ed.). Continuum.

Freire, P. (2004). *Pedagogy of hope: Reliving pedagogy of oppressed*. Continuum.

Freire, P. (2005). *Teachers as cultural workers: Letters to those who dare teach*. Routledge.

Freire, P., & Macedo, D. (1987). *Literacy: Reading the word and the world*. Bergin & Garvey.

Fuligni, A. (Ed.) (2007). *Contesting stereotypes and creating identities*. Russell Sage Foundation.

Ganz, M. L. (2009). *What is public narrative: Self, us & now*. Harvard. https://dash.harvard.edu/handle/1/30760283

García, S. B., & Guerra, P. L. (2004). Deconstructing deficit thinking: Working with educators to create more equitable learning environments. *Education and Urban Society*, 36(2), 150–68.

García-Carrión, R., López de aguileta, G., Padrós, M., & Ramis-Salas, M. (2020). Implications for social impact of dialogic teaching and learning. *Frontiers in Psychology*, 11, 140.

García-Carrión, R., Padrós Cuxart, M., Alvarez, P., & Flecha, A. (2020). Teacher induction in schools as learning communities: Successful pathways to teachers' professional development in a diverse school serving students living in poverty. *Sustainability*, 12(17), 7146.

Garthwaite, K. (2016). Stigma, shame and "people like us": An ethnographic study of foodbank use in the UK. *The Journal of Poverty and Social Justice: Research, Policy, Practice*, 24(3), 277–89. https://doi.org/10.1332/175982716X14721954314922

Gazeley, L. (2019). Unpacking "disadvantage" and "potential" in the context of fair access policies in England. *Educational Review*, 71(6), 673–90.

Gómez, J. & Vargas, J. (2003). Why Romà do not like mainstream schools: Voices of a people without territory. *Harvard Educational Review*, 73(4), 559–90.

Gonski, D., Arcus, T., Boston, K., Gould, V., Johnson, W., O'Brien, L., Perry, L., & Roberts, M. (2018). *Through growth to achievement: The report of the review to achieve educational excellence in Australian schools*. Commonwealth of Australia.

Gorski, P. C. (2008). Peddling poverty for profit: Elements of oppression in Ruby Payne's framework. *Equity & Excellence in Education*, 41(1), 130–48.

Gorski, P. C. (2016). Equity literacy: More than celebrating diversity. *Diversity in Education*, 11(1), 12–14. http://www. edchange.org/publications/Equity-Literacy-More-than-Celebrating-Diversity.pdf

Gorur, R. (2011). Policy as assemblage. *European Educational Research Journal*, 10(4), 611–22. https://doi.org/10.2304/eerj.2011.10.4.611

Goward, P. (2021, October 19). Why you shouldn't underestimate the underclass. *The Financial Review*. https://www.afr.com/policy/economy/don-t-underestimate-the-underclass-20211018-p5910c

Graham, H., Minhas, R., & Paxton, G. (2016). Learning problems in children of refugee background: A systematic review. *Pediatrics*, 137(6), 1–15. https://doi.org/10.1542/peds.2015-3994

Grossman, P., & Dean, C. G. P. (2019). Negotiating a common language and shared understanding about core practices: The case of discussion. *Teaching and Teacher Education*, 80, 157–66.

Habermas, J. (1987). *The theory of communicative action: Lifeworld and systems, a critique of functionalist reason*. Polity Press.

Hall, J. (2000). It hurts to be a girl: Growing up poor, white, and female. *Gender & Society*, 14(5), 630–43. https://doi.org/10.1177/089124300014005003

Harris, A., & Marlowe, J. (2011). Hard yards and high hopes: The educational challenges of African refugee university students. *Australian International Journal of Teaching and Learning in Higher Education*, 23(2), 186–96.

Hayes, A., Gray, M., & Edwards, B. (2008). *Social inclusion: Origins, concepts and key themes*. Social Inclusion Unit, Department of the Prime Minister and Cabinet.

Heimans, S., Singh, P., & Barnes, A. (2021). Researching educational disadvantage: Concepts emerging from working in/with an Australian school. *Improving Schools*, 24(2), 182–92.

Helliwell, J., Layard, R., Sachs, J., & De Neve, J. (Eds.). *World Happiness Report 2021*. Sustainable Development Solutions Network.

Hogarth, M. (2017). Speaking back to the deficit discourses: A theoretical and methodological approach. *Australian Educational Research*, 44(1), 21–34.

Howard, T. (2010). *Why race and culture matter in schools: Closing the achievement gap in America's classrooms.* Teachers College Press.

Huggins, J. (1989). *Sister girl: Reflections on Tiddaism, identity and reconciliation.* University of Queensland Press.

Huilla, H. (2022). *Kaupunkikoulut ja huono-osaisuus [Ubran schools and disadvantage].* Yliopistopaino Unigrafia.

Jayawardena, K. (1986). *Feminism and nationalism in the third world.* Zed Books.

Kallio, J., & Hakovirta, M. (2020). *Lapsiperheiden köyhyys & huono-osaisuus [Poverty and disadvantage of families with children].* Vastapaino.

Kane, E. W. (2019). Maximum feasible participation and paternalistic culture of poverty approaches: Tensions in commodified poverty reduction curricula. *Journal of Poverty*, 23(5), 437–55.

Kaukko, M. (2021). Storycrafting refugee children's lives. Presenting Ali and the long journey to Australia. *International Journal of Qualitative Studies in Education.* https://doi.org/10.1080/095183 98.2021.1986645

Kaukko, M., & Wilkinson, J. (2020). Learning how to go on: Refugee students and informal learning practices. *International Journal of Inclusive Education*, 24(11), 1175–93. https://doi.org/ 10.1080/13603116.2018.1514080

Kaukko, M., Wilkinson, J., & Kohli, R. (2022). Pedagogical love in Finland and Australia: A study of refugee children and their teachers. *Pedagogy, Culture and Society* 30(5), 731–47. https:// doi.org/10.1080/14681366.2020.1868555

Kellaghan, T. (2001). Towards a definition of educational disadvantage. *The Irish Journal of Education/Iris Eireannach an Oideachais*, 32, 3–22. http://www.jstor.org/stable/30076741

Kemmis, S. (2012). Researching educational praxis: Spectator and participant perspectives. *British Educational Research Journal*, 38(6), 885–905. https://doi.org/10.1080/01411926.2011.588316

Kemmis, S., Wilkinson, J., Edwards-Groves, C., Hardy, I., Grootenboer, P., & Bristol, L. (2014). *Changing practices, changing education.* Springer.

Koch, K. A. (2020). The voice of the parent cannot be undervalued: Pre-service teachers' observations after listening to the experiences of parents of students with disabilities. *Societies*, 10(3), 50. https://doi.org/10.3390/soc10030050

Koksvik, O., & Øverland, G. (2019). Profiting from poverty. *Canadian Journal of Philosophy*, 49(3), 341–67.

Kretchmar, Sondel B., & Ferrare, J. J. (2018). The power of the network: Teach for America's impact on the deregulation of teacher education. *Educational Policy*, 32(3), 423–53.

Ladson-Billings, G. (1994). *The dreamkeepers: Successful teachers of African American children*. John Wiley & Sons.

Lampert, J. (2020). A community-engaged framework for the preparation of teachers for high-poverty communities. *Australian Educational Researcher*, 48(3), 449–66. https://doi.org/10.1007/s13384-020-00406-8

Lampert, J., & Browne, S. (2022). Examining teacher candidates' backgrounds, experiences, and beliefs as precursors for developing dispositions for democracy. *Teachers College Record (1970)*, 124(3), 148–76. https://doi.org/10.1177/01614681221086995

Lawton, W. (2020). "Struggle street": Re-staging the private for public consumption. *Limina: A Journal of Historical and Cultural Studies*, 26(1), 40–52. https://www.limina.arts.uwa.edu.au/__data/assets/pdf_file/0010/3646747/Limina-26-1_04_Lawton_Struggle-Street.pdf

Lefebvre, E. E., & Thomas, M. (2017). "Shit shows" or "like-minded schools": Charter schools and the neoliberal logic of Teach for America. *Journal of Education Policy*, 32(3), 357–71.

Lewis, L. F., Ward, C., Jarvis, N., & Cawley, E. (2020). "Straight sex is complicated enough!": The lived experiences of autistics who are gay, lesbian, bisexual, asexual, or other sexual orientations. *Journal of Autism and Developmental Disorders*, 51(7), 2324–37. https://doi.org/10.1007/s10803-020-04696-w

Lingard, B., & Keddie, A. (2013). Redistribution, recognition and representation: Working against pedagogies of indifference. *Pedagogy, Culture & Society*, 21(3), 427–47.

Lockhart, Z. (2019). Mutual vulnerability and intergenerational healing: Black women HBCU students writing memoir. *Journal of Poetry Therapy*, 32(3), 169–80. https://doi.org/10.1080/08893675.2019.1625156

López, F. A. (2016). Culturally responsive pedagogies in Arizona and Latino students' achievement. *Teachers College Record*, 118(5), 1–42.

Luguetti, C., & Oliver, K. L. (2019). "I became a teacher that respects the kids' voices": Challenges and facilitators pre-service teachers faced in learning an activist approach. *Sport, Education and Society*. https://doi.org/10.1080/13573322.2019.1601620

Macedo, D. (1994). *Literacies of power: What Americans are not allowed to know*. Westview Press, Inc.

Mahon, K., Heikkinen, H. & Huttunen, R. (2019). Critical educational praxis in university ecosystems: Enablers and constraints, *Pedagogy, Culture & Society*, 27(3), 463–80.

Major, J., Wilkinson, J., Santoro, N., & Langat, K. (2013). Sudanese young people of refugee background in rural and regional Australia: Social capital and education success. *Australian and International Journal of Rural Education*, 23(3), 95–105.

Manso, J. (2019). *La formación inicial del profesorado en España: análisis de los planes de estudios tras una década desde su implementación. Ministerio de Educación y Formación Profesional*. [Initial teacher training in Spain: Analysis of the study plans after a decade since its implementation. Ministry of Education and Vocational Training].

May, V. M. (2015). *Pursuing intersectionality, Unsettling dominant imaginaries*. Routledge.

McLachlan, R., Gilfillan, G., & Gordon, J. (2013). *Deep and persistent disadvantage in Australia* (Staff working paper). Productivity Commission.

McLeod, J., & Wright, J. (2016). What does wellbeing do? An approach to defamiliarize keywords in youth studies. *Journal of Youth Studies*, 9(6), 776–92.

McNew-Birren, J., Hildebrand, T., & Belknap, G. (2017). Strange bedfellows in science teacher preparation: Conflicting perspectives on social justice presented in a Teach for America–university partnership. *Cultural Studies of Science Education*, 13(2), 437–62.

Milner IV, H. R. (2014). Research on classroom management in urban schools. In E. Edmund (Ed.), *Handbook of classroom management* (pp. 177–95). Routledge.

Milner, H. R. (2013). Why are students of color (still) punished more severely and frequently than white students? *Urban Education*, 48(4), 483–9.

Mockler, N. (2022). Teacher professional learning under audit: Reconfiguring practice in an age of standards. *Professional Development in Education*, 48(1), 166–80.

Moll, L. C., Amanti, C., Neff, D., & González, N. (1992). Funds of knowledge for teaching: Using a qualitative approach to connect homes and classrooms. *Theory into Practice* 31(2), 132–41. http://www.jstor.org/stable/1476399

Moll, L., & Gonzalez, N. (1997). Teachers as social scientists: Learning about culture from household research. In P. M. Hall (Ed.), *Race, ethnicity and multiculturalism: Missouri symposium on research and educational policy* (vol. 1, p. 89114). Garland.

Moodie, N., & Patrick, R. (2017). Settler grammars and the Australian professional standards for teachers. *Asia-Pacific Journal of Teacher Education*, 45(5), 439–54.

Moodie, N., Vass, G., & Lowe, K. (2021). The Aboriginal voices project: Findings and reflections. *Asia-Pacific Journal of Teacher Education*, 49(1), 5–19.

Moreton-Robinson, A. (2020). *Talkin' up to the white woman: Indigenous women and feminism* (20th anniversary ed.). University of Queensland Press.

Morrice, L. (2009). Journeys into higher education: The case of refugees in the UK. *Teaching in Higher Education*, 14(6), 661–72.

Muniz, J. (2019). Culturally responsive teaching: A 50-state survey of teaching standards. *New America*. newamerica.org/education-policy/reports/culturally-responsive-teaching/

Naidoo, L. (2015). Imagination and aspiration: Flames of possibility for migrant background high school students and their parents. *Australian Journal of Teacher Education*, 40(3), 101–15.

Naidoo, L., & Adoniou, M. (2019). "I speak 19 languages": Accessing the linguistic and cultural resources of students from refugee backgrounds. *The European Journal of Applied Linguistics and TEFL*, 8(1), 111–30.

Naidoo, L., Wilkinson, J., Langat, K., Adoniou, M., Cunneen, R., & Bolger, D. (2015). *Case study report: Supporting school-university pathways for refugee students' access and participation in tertiary education*. Western Sydney University. http://www.uws.edu.au/__ data/assets/pdf_file/0011/830864/Case_Study_Report.pdf

Naidoo, L., Wilkinson, J., Adoniou, M., & Langat, A. (2018). *Refugee background students transitioning into higher education: Navigating complex spaces*. Springer. https://doi. org/10.1007/978-981-13-0420-0

Nuttall, A., & Beckett, L. (2020). Teachers' professional knowledge work on poverty and disadvantage. In L. Beckett (Ed.), *Research-informed teacher learning: Critical perspectives on theory, research and practice* (pp. 149–63). Routledge.

Pallotta-Chiarolli, M., & Rajkhowa, A. (2017). Systemic invisibilities, institutional culpabilities and multi-cultural-multi-faith LGBTIQ resistances, *Journal of Intercultural Studies*, 38(4), 429–42, DOI: 10.1080/07256868.2017.1341013

Payne, R. (2006). *Bridges out of poverty*. Aha! Press.

Payne, R. (2018). *Understanding and working with students and adults from poverty*. Aha! Press. www.ahaprocess.com

Peercy, M. M., Tigert, J., Fredricks, D., Kidwell, T., Feagin, K., Hall, W., … & Lawyer, M. D. (2022). From humanizing principles to humanizing practices: Exploring core practices as a bridge to enacting humanizing pedagogy with multilingual students. *Teaching and Teacher Education*, 113, 103653.

Peltola, M., Huilla, H., Luoma, T., & Oittinen, R. (2023). Everyday life in schools in disadvantaged areas. In: Thrupp, M., Seppänen, P., Kauko, J., Kosunen, S. (Eds.), *Finland's famous education system* (pp. 211–25). Singapore: Springer.

Phillips, B., & Narayanan, V. (2020). *Financial stress and social security settings in Australia*. ANU Centre for Social Research and Methods, Australian National University.

Power, S., Curtis, A., Whitty, G., & Edwards, T. (2010). Private education and disadvantage: The experiences of assisted place holders. *International Studies in Sociology of Education*, 20(1), 23–38.

Price-Robertson, R. (2021). What is community disadvantage: Understanding the issues, overcoming the problem. *Communities and Families Clearinghouse Australia*. https://aifs.gov.au/resources/policy-and-practice-papers/ what-community-disadvantage-understanding-issues-overcoming#:~:text=Community%20disadvantage%20

comes%20about%20as,%2C%20relative%20lack%20of%20op-
portunities

Raffo, C. (2011). Barker's ecology of disadvantage and educational
equity: Issues of redistribution and recognition. *Journal of
Educational Administration and History*, 43(4), 325–43.

Robinson, D., & Goodey, C. (2018). Agency in the darkness: "Fear
of the unknown", learning disability and teacher education for
inclusion. *International Journal of Inclusive Education*, 22(4),
426–40. https://doi.org/10.1080/13603116.2017.1370738

Robinson, M. (2020). Practical learning for ethical agency in
teaching. In Edwards, N., Robinson, Maureen, & America,
Carina (Eds.), *Teacher education for transformative agency:
Critical perspectives on design, content and pedagogy*. South
Africa: University of the Free State.

Rowan, L., Mayer, D., Kline, J., Kostogriz, A., & Walker-Gibbs, B.
(2014). Investigating the effectiveness of teacher education for
early career teachers in diverse settings: The longitudinal research
we have to have. *Australian Educational Researcher*, 42(3),
273–98.

Rowe, E., & Perry, L. (2019). Private financing in urban public
schools: Inequalities in a stratified education marketplace.
Australian Educational Researcher, 47(1), 19–37. https://doi.
org/10.1007/s13384-019-00328-0

Saari, J. (2015). *Huono-osaiset: elämän edellytykset yhteiskunnan
pohjalla*. Gaudeamus.

Sahlberg, P. (2011). *Finnish lessons: what can the world learn from
educational change in Finland?* Teachers College Press.

Salmi, M. (2020). Lapsiperheiden köyhyys pitää yllä köyhyyden
kierrettä [Poverty of families with children maintains a circle of
poverty]. In J. Kallio & M. Hakovirta (Eds.), *Lapsiperheiden
köyhyys & huono-osaisuus [Poverty and disadvantage of families
with children]* (pp. 37–72). Vastapaino.

Salter, P., & Maxwell, J. (2016). The inherent vulnerability of the
Australian Curriculum's cross-curriculum priorities. *Critical
Studies in Education*, 57(3), 296–312.

Salton, Y., Riddle, S., & Baguley, M. (2022). The "good" teacher in
an era of professional standards: Policy frameworks and lived
realities. *Teachers and Teaching, Theory and Practice*, 28(1),
51–63.

Santiago-Garabieta, M., García-Carrión, R., Zubiri-Esnaola, H., & López de Aguileta, G. (2021). Inclusion of L2 (Basque) learners in dialogic literary gatherings in a linguistically diverse context. *Language Teaching Research*, 1362168821994142.

Santoro, N., & Kennedy, A. (2016). How is cultural diversity positioned in teacher professional standards? An international analysis. *Asia-Pacific Journal of Teacher Education*, 44(3), 208–23.

Santoro, N., & Wilkinson, J. (2015). Sudanese young people building capital in rural Australia: The role of mothers and community. *Ethnography and Education*, 11(1), 107–20. https://doi.org/10.1080/17457823.2015.1073114

Sensoy, O., & DiAngelo, R. (2017). *Is everyone really equal? An introduction to key concepts in social justice education* (2nd ed.). Teachers College Press.

Severs, E., Celis, K., & Erzeel, S. (2016). Power, privilege and disadvantage: Intersectionality theory and political representation. *Politics*, 36(4), 346–54.

Shay, M., Woods, A., & Sarra, G. (2019, August 14). The imagination declaration: Young Indigenous Australians want to be heard—but will we listen? *The Sector*. https://thesector.com.au/2019/08/14/the-imagination-declaration-young-indigenous-australians-want-to-be-heard-but-will-we-listen/

Simmons-Horton, S. Y. (2020). "A Bad combination": Lived experiences of youth involved in the foster care and juvenile justice systems. *Child & Adolescent Social Work Journal*, 38(6), 583–97. https://doi.org/10.1007/s10560-020-00693-1

Simpson, A. (2016). Dialogic teaching in the initial teacher education classroom: "Everyone's Voice will be Heard". *Research Papers in Education*, 31(1), 89–106.

Skidmore, D. (2006). Pedagogy and dialogue. *Cambridge Journal of Education*, 36(4), 503–14.

Smit, R. (2012). Towards a clearer understanding of student disadvantage in higher education: Problematising deficit thinking. *Higher Education Research & Development*, 31(3), 369–80.

Smith, C., & Hope, E. (2020). "We just want to break the stereotype": Tensions in Black boys' critical social analysis of their suburban school experiences. *Journal of Educational Psychology*, 112(3), 551–66. https://eric.ed.gov/?id=EJ1247194

Smith, G., & Smith, T. (2014). Targeting educational disadvantage by area: Continuity and change in urban areas in England, 1968–2014. *Oxford Review of Education*, 40(6), 715–38.

Smyth, J. (2012). The socially just school and critical pedagogies in communities put at a disadvantage. *Critical Studies in Education*, 53(1), 9–18.

Soler, M. (2015). Biographies of "invisible" people who transform their lives and enhance social transformations through dialogic gatherings. *Qualitative Inquiry*, 21(10), 839–42.

South African Council of Educators (SACE). *Professional teaching standards*.

Spring, N. (2007). Tracing the language of educational disadvantage. In P. Downes & A. L. Gilligan (Eds.), *Beyond educational disadvantage* (pp. 3–9). Institute of Public Administration.

Steinberg, S., & Krumer-Nevo, M. (2022). Poverty-aware teacher education. *European Journal of Teacher Education*, 45(2), 266–81. https://doi.org/10.1080/02619768.2020.1827390

Stromquist, N. P. (2014). Freire, literacy and emancipatory gender learning. *International Review of Education*, 60(4), 545–58. https://doi.org/10.1007/s11159-014-9424-2

Taylor, J., Wyn, Johanna, & Brotherhood of St. Laurence issuing body. (2014). *Life chances: Stories of growing up in Australia*. Annandale, NSW: Federation Press.

Taylor, K.-Y. (2017). *How we get free: Black feminism and the Combahee River Collective*. Haymarket Books.

Teach for All (n.d.). *Home*. https://teachforall.org/

Teaching Council (2016). *Code of professional conduct for teachers* (2nd ed.). Ireland: Teaching Council. https://www.teachingcouncil.ie/en/fitness-to-teach/updated-code-of-professional-conduct/

Teaching Service Commission (2017). *Professional standards for teachers and school leaders in Sierra Leone*.

Terry, L., Naylor, R., Nguyen, N., & Rizzo, A. (2016). *Not there yet: An investigation into the access and participation of students from humanitarian refugee backgrounds in the Australian higher education system*. National Centre for Student Equity in Higher Education. https://www.ncsehe.edu.au/publications/an-investigation-into-the-participation-of-students-of-refugee-backgrounds-in-the-australian-higher-education-system/

Thomas, A. S. (2018). *Dangerous mindsets: An analysis of white lady bountiful in teach for America*. ProQuest Dissertations Publishing.

Thomas, M., Rauschenberger, E., & Crawford-Garrett, K. (2021). *Examining teach for all: International perspectives on a growing global network*. Routledge.

Thomas, P. L. (2010). The Payne of addressing race and poverty in public education: Utopian accountability and deficit assumptions of middle-class America. *Souls*, 12(3), 262–83.

Thompson, I. (2017). *Tackling social disadvantage through teacher education*. Critical Publishing Ltd.

Thompson, I., & Menter, I. (2017). Language, literacy and disadvantage. In I. Thompson (Ed.), *Tackling social disadvantage through teacher education*. Critical Publishing.

Thorpe, K., Burgess, C., & Egan, S. (2021). Aboriginal community-led preservice teacher education: Learning from country in the city. *The Australian Journal of Teacher Education*, 46(1), 55–73.

Thrupp, M., Seppänen, P., Kauko, J., Kosunen, S. (2023). *Finland's famous education system: Unvarnished insights into Finnish schooling*. Springer.

Tsolidis, G. (1986). Educating Voula: A report on non-English speaking background girls and education. (Prepared for the Ministerial Advisory Committee on Multicultural and Migrant Education). *Ministry of Education Victoria*. https://catalogue.nla.gov.au/Record/2198885

Tuhiwai Smith, L. (1999). *Decolonizing methodologies: Research and Indigenous peoples*. Zed Books.

United Nations High Commission for Refugees (UNHCR) (n.d.). *Education*. https://www.unhcr.org/en-au/education.html

United Nations High Commission for Refugees (UNHCR) (2022a). *Refugee data finder*. https://www.unhcr.org/refugee-statistics

United Nations High Commission for Refugees (UNHCR) (2022b). *Tertiary education*. https://www.unhcr.org/en-au/tertiary-education.html

Uptin, J. (2021). "If I peel off my Black skin maybe then I integrate". Examining how African-Australian youth find living in a "post multicultural" Australia. *Social Identities*, 27(1), 75–91, https://doi.org/10.1080/13504630.2020.1814726

Valencia, R. R. (2010). *Dismantling contemporary deficit thinking: Educational thought and practice*. Routledge.

Vargas, J., & Gómez, J. (2003). Why Romà do not like mainstream schools: Voices of a people without territory. *Harvard Educational Review*, 73(4), 559–90.

Vernikoff, L., Goodwin, A., Horn, C., & Akin, S. (2022). Urban residents' place-based funds of knowledge: An untapped resource in urban teacher residencies. *Urban Education*, 57(1), 32–57. https://doi.org/10.1177/0042085918801887

Victorian Institute of Teaching (2010). *Standards for graduating teachers*. http://www.vit.vic.edu.au/SiteCollectionDocuments/PDF/Standards-for-Graduating-Teachersjan-09.pdf

Vinson, T. (2009). *Social inclusion: Markedly socially disadvantaged localities in Australia: Their nature and possible remediation*. Department of Education, Employment and Workplace Relations.

Webb, S., Dunwoodie, K., Wilkinson, J., Macaulay, L., Reimer, K., & Kaukko, M. (2021). Recognition and precarious mobilities: The experiences of university students from a refugee background in Australia. *International Review of Education*, 67, 871–94. https://doi.org/10.1007/s11159-021-09919-5

Weiler, K. (1991). Freire and a feminist pedagogy of difference. *Harvard Educational Review*, 61(4), 449–74. https://doi.org/10.17763/haer.61.4.a102265jl68rju84

Western Sydney University (WSU) News Centre (2021, March 26). *Western Sydney University professor leading review into NSW government complaints process*. https://www.westernsydney.edu.au/newscentre/news_centre/more_news_stories/western_sydney_university_professor_leading_review_into_nsw_government_complaints_process

Western Sydney University (WSU) (n.d.-a). *About us*. https://www.westernsydney.edu.au/publicaccessinformation/agency_information_guide/about_us

Western Sydney University (WSU) (n.d.-b). *Strategic plan*. https://www.westernsydney.edu.au/about_uws/leadership/strategic_plan

Western Sydney University (WSU) (n.d.-c). *Western's admission profile*. https://www.westernsydney.edu.au/future/study/how-to-apply/admission-transparency-information/woi-admissions-profile

Westover, T. (2018). *Educated*. Random House.

Westover, T. (2019). Inequality by degrees [Review]. *New York Times Book Review*, 15–15. The New York Times Company.

Wilkinson, J. (2018). Navigating the terrain of higher education. In L. Naidoo, J. Wilkinson, M. Adoniou, & K. Langat (Eds.), *Refugee background students transitioning into higher education: Navigating complex spaces* (pp. 89–110). Springer. https://doi.org/10.1007/978-981-13-0420-0

Wilkinson, J., & Langat, K. (2012). Exploring educators' practices for African students from refugee backgrounds in an Australian regional high school. *The Australasian Review of African Studies*, 33(2), 158–77.

Wilkinson, J., & Lloyd-Zantiotis, A. (2017). The role of everyday spaces for learning for refugee youth. In R. Elmeksy, C. Camp Yeakey, & O. Marcucci (Eds.), *The power of resistance: Culture, ideology and social reproduction in global contexts* (pp. 383–408). Emerald Press. https://doi.org/10.1108/s1479-358x20140000012018

Wilkinson, J., & MacDonald, K. (2022). Gender, educational leadership and social justice: An intersectional lens. In V. Showunmi, P. Moorosi, C. Shakeshaft, & I. Oplatka (Eds.), *The Bloomsbury handbook of gender and educational leadership and management* (pp. 90–100). Bloomsbury Publishing.

Wilkinson, J., Santoro, N., & Major, J. (2017). Sudanese refugee youth and educational success: The role of church and youth group in supporting cultural and academic adjustment and schooling achievement. *International Journal of Intercultural Relations*, 60, 210–9. https://doi.org/10.1016/j.ijintrel.2017.04.003

Williams, R. (1985). *Keywords: A vocabulary of culture and society*. Oxford University Press.

Wolff, J., & De-Shalit, A. (2007). *Disadvantage*. Oxford University Press.

Wrigley, T. (2019). The problem of reductionism in educational theory: Complexity, causality, values. *Power and Education*, 11(2), 145–62.

Yarbrough, D. (2020). "Nothing about us without us": Reading protests against oppressive knowledge production as guidelines for solidarity research. *Journal of Contemporary Ethnography*, 49(1), 58–85. https://doi.org/10.1177/0891241619857134

Yuval-Davis, N. (2011). *The politics of belonging: Intersectional contestations*. SAGE.

Zeichner, K., Bowman, M., Guillen, L., & Napolitan, K. (2016). Engaging and working in solidarity with local communities in preparing the teachers of their children. *Journal of Teacher Education*, 67(4), 277–90.

Zhang, D., Katsiyannis, A., Ju, S., & Roberts, E. (2014). Minority representation in special education: 5-year trends. *Journal of Child and Family Studies*, 23(1), 118–27.

Zygmunt, E., Cipollone, K., Clark, P., & Tancock, S. (2022). Community-engaged teacher preparation. *Oxford Research Encyclopedia of Education*. https://doi.org/10.1093/acrefore/9780190264093.013.476

INDEX